P9-DDF-195

Shonie B. Levi received her education at Teachers Institute of the Jewish Theological Seminary, Cooper Union Art School, and Columbia University. She has taken a leading role in many phases of Jewish life; she is a member of the national boards of the National Women's League of the United Synagogue of America and of Hadassah. Mrs. Levi is a radio commentator, lecturer, and educator. She is the wife of Rabbi S. Gershon Levi, spiritual leader of the Jamaica Jewish Center, and she is the mother of a son and daughter.

The late Sylvia R. Kaplan was graduated from Hunter College. She edited books and wrote articles in various fields and served as a consultant in printing and publishing. In the field of Jewish service, she was active in her synagogue sisterhood, Hadassah, and the National Council of Jewish Women. Mrs. Kaplan was the wife of Dr. Lawrence G. Kaplan and mother of a daughter.

Guide for
the Jewish Homemaker

Guide *for*
the Jewish Homemaker

SHONIE B. LEVI

SYLVIA R. KAPLAN

SCHOCKEN BOOKS · NEW YORK

Illustrated by Jessie B. Robinson

Copyright © 1959, 1964 by Shonie B. Levi and Sylvia R. Kaplan

All rights reserved under International and Pan-American
Copyright Conventions. Published in the United States
by Schocken Books Inc., New York. Distributed by
Pantheon Books, a division of Random House, Inc., New York.

Library of Congress Catalog Card Number 59-12039
ISBN 0-8052-0087-8

Manufactured in the United States of America

Revised Schocken edition published in 1978

B 9 8 7

TO OUR MOTHERS
AND OUR DAUGHTERS

To the place my heart loves,
my feet carry me

HILLEL

Contents

Foreword

THIS BOOK IS ADDRESSED to the woman who wants to run a Jewish household, be she wife, mother or bride-to-be. We have felt that there is a need for a single volume which will provide her with all the basic techniques of Jewish home-making.

We have not, by any means, attempted to write a treatise on Jewish religion, history or theology, nor to produce a *shulhan aruh*. But we have provided a measure of interpretive background, to give significance to family observance and ceremonials in the home and synagogue. It is our hope that those passages will lead to further study.

For this reason, we have added a list of related reading at the end of each chapter, as well as a more general bibliography at the end of the book. For quick and easy reference, we have also appended an abridged calendar of festivals, some of the shorter prayers used in the home and other useful data.

Nor have we ignored some of the more general aspects of house-wifery; we have dealt with such matters as home economics and family recreation, and suggested good reading in these fields.

How to Use This Book

The table of contents should guide you to the broad topics under discussion—the festivals, the dietary laws, the education of children, the economics of homemaking, and so on. But if you want to look up a specific detail, consult the index at the back of the book.

Our subject matter requires us to use many Hebrew, and some Yiddish words. We do not believe it is possible to devise one universal system of transliteration which will serve every purpose. For our purposes, we have adopted the following rules:

Words, whatever their origin, which are frequently used in English, are given their common spelling, and treated as English words—Torah, kosher, Yom Kippur, and so on. Arbitrarily, we treat all the festivals in the same way. All other Hebrew words are italicized, and transliterated with the so-called Sephardic pronunciation in mind. *Alef* and *ayin* are ignored. *Vet* and *vav* are both indicated by "*v*"; *tet* and *tav* by "*t*"; *kaf* and *kof* by "*k*." The properly differing sounds of *het* and *haf* are both rendered as "*h*." *Tzaddi* is shown as "*tz*," and two consecutive vowels are separated by an apostrophe. To indicate the vowel-murmur of the sounded *sheva*, we use the letter "*e*."

We know that none of this is scientific, but we hope that scholars will bear with us. After all, our aim is not academic.

As for Yiddish words, we have simply rendered them as phonetically as we know how, and placed them in quotation marks.

All non-English terms are explained in their main context. But of course you may run across them elsewhere in the book, and want to know their meaning. Simply turn to the glossary at the back, as you would to a dictionary.

Acknowledgments

If our list of thank you's is a long one, that is because so many have been kind to us in so many ways.

Our thanks go to the National Women's League of the United Synagogue of America for giving us its official encouragement; and to those of its members who read the manuscript and discussed it with us: to the president, Mrs. H. Herbert Rossman; to the past presidents, Mrs. Barnett E. Kopelman, Mrs. Emanuel Siner, Mrs. Louis Sussman; and to the members of the Reading

Committee, Mrs. Ben Zion Bokser, Mrs. Sylvan H. Kohn, Mrs. Josiah Derby, Mrs. Louis Ginzberg, Mrs. Simon Greenberg, Mrs. Alexander Marx, Mrs. Judah Nadich, Mrs. Charles Schwartz, Mrs. Saul Teplitz, Mrs. Baruch I. Treiger, and to Miss Naomi Flax.

We are most grateful to those scholars who gave us guidance: Rabbi Abraham E. Millgram, director of the United Synagogue Commission on Jewish Education; Rabbi Arthur Neulander, chairman of the Law Committee of the Rabbinical Assembly; Rabbi Marvin Wiener, director of the National Academy for Adult Jewish Studies of the United Synagogue of America; Dr. Azriel Eisenberg executive vice-president of the Jewish Education Committee of New York; Dr. Stephen S. Kayser, curator of the Jewish Museum.

Experts in various fields were most generous in sharing their experience: we thank Mrs. D. Leonard Cohen, vice-president, National Hadassah; Miss Miriam R. Ephraim, program director, National Jewish Welfare Board; Mrs. Judith Kaplan Eisenstein, author and musicologist; Mrs. Max Gelb, consultant in Jewish education; Mrs. Temima Gezari, art director, Jewish Education Committee; Miss Leah M. Jaffa, music director, National Jewish Welfare Board; Mrs. Meyer Rotenberg, Canadian lecturer and radio commentator; Mr. Ralph Bahn, Budget Director, Department of Hospitals, Washington, D. C.; and, for her interest and encouragement, Mrs. Barnett Janner, J. P., member of British Board of Deputies.

Rabbi Simon Greenberg, Vice Chancellor of the Jewish Theological Seminary, was especially encouraging; his enthusiasm for the project led us to see it through.

We owe a very special kind of thanks to our dear friend Mrs. Arthur Minsky, who spent endless hours typing and retyping the manuscript; to our loving and patient families for their indulgence through months of research, writing and conferences.

Finally we want to thank Rabbi S. Gershon Levi, without whose guidance and help in form as well as content this book could not have been written.

S.B.L.
S.R.K.

Introduction

"Many daughters have done valiantly"
(Proverbs 31:29)

THE BUSINESS OF BEING A HOUSEWIFE can be looked at in two ways. It can be viewed as a series of chores—cooking, baking, cleaning, washing, shopping, getting the children off to school, keeping a husband well fed and comfortable. On the other hand, it can be thought of as a vocation of the highest significance—the vocation of homemaker. Lived in these terms, it becomes a calling devoted to the very fabric of life itself. Health and happiness, faith and the molding of character, love, religion, parenthood, birth, marriage, bereavement, consolation—for these essentials of life the family is home base. And in all these, the homemaker has a key role to play.

Indeed, her role is a many-sided one. She must be wife, nurse, mother, cook, confidante, teacher, diplomat, economist, companion, interior decorator, hostess. She can scarcely expect to have professional *expertise* in all of these fields; fortunately for her, and for the human race, she does not have to. There are experts to serve her and guide her. The butcher and baker and candlestick maker, the physician, the clergyman, the educator, the nutritionist, the merchant and a host of others are at her beck and call. A whole shelf of books on the modern arts and sciences of homemaking is available to her, and will form a part of the equipment of a modern housewife, as important to her, at the very least, as her pots and pans and household appliances.

Her most important equipment, of course, is none of these, but rather her own self; her personality, her intelligence, her womanly maturity, her patience, her upbringing, her sense of values. It is in her hands that the various strands converge. It is for her—together with her husband, naturally—to weave them into the integrated design that will give her family its character, in a pattern of creative homemaking.

In the truly Jewish home, creative homemaking calls for special skills, special knowledge—and offers special rewards. For Judaism is a home-centered way of life. The Sabbaths and the Festivals are observed at their deepest and most meaningful level in the bosom of the family. In Jewish tradition, the home is called *mikdash me'at*, a miniature sanctuary; the family table is designated an altar. The Jewish heritage finds its fullest expression in the home.

Generations of mothers and grandmothers have passed the tradition of Jewish homemaking on to their daughters. It is to provide a practical guide to this tradition, as it can be continued and enriched in the conditions of modern living, that this book has been written.

In writing it, the authors have coped admirably with the problem of selection in a field whose ramifications are almost endless. And if "woman's work is never done," it is equally in order to ask "Where does it begin?" This question, too, the authors have answered wisely, for themselves and for their readers. They have chosen to start at the threshold. For even before you open the door of the Jewish home, you see the mezuzah, a reminder that the home is intended to be a sanctuary, and that the job of its presiding genius, the wife and mother, is essentially a spiritual one.

S. GERSHON LEVI

CHAPTER 1

Across the Threshold

"Every wise woman buildeth her house" (Proverbs 14:1)

1

Across the Threshold

A S YOU COME TO THE DOOR of a Jewish home, the very doorpost
tells a story. There, on the right side as you enter, is a small
case attached to the upper third of the doorpost, usually
in a slanting position. This is the mezuzah, one of the symbols of
the Jewish way of life.

Visible, perhaps through a small opening, perhaps on the case
itself, is the Hebrew word *shaddai* (Almighty) or its initial letter
ש . But you will find the mezuzah itself is inside the case. It
consists of a small parchment scroll, containing two paragraphs
from the Torah: *shema* (Deuteronomy 6:4-9); and *vehayah im
shamo'a* (Deuteronomy 11:13-21).

These two paragraphs constitute the ancient core of Jewish
daily prayer, the Jew's declaration of faith. They stress the love of
the one God, and of the Torah as a way of life. Each paragraph
also contains the command "Write them [i.e., these words] on the
doorposts of your house, and upon your gates."

A MARK OF DISTINCTION

THE NAME OF THIS little parchment scroll is simply the Hebrew
word for "doorpost." Its contents are teachings of Judaism. Clearly
then, the mezuzah is intended as a lesson, not as a charm.

SHEMA

Hear, O Israel, the Lord our God, the Lord is One.
And thou shalt love the Lord thy God with all thy heart,
  with all thy soul, and with all thy might.
And these words which I command thee this day shall be
  upon thy heart.
And thou shalt teach them diligently unto thy children,
  and shalt talk of them when thou sittest in thy house,
  and when thou walkest by the way, and when thou
  liest down, and when thou risest up.
And thou shalt bind them for a sign upon thy hand, and
  they shall be for frontlets between thine eyes.
And thou shalt write them upon the doorposts of thy
  house and upon thy gates.

Deuteronomy 6:4-9

PUTTING UP THE MEZUZAH   The Jewish bride entering her home is spiritually, as well as literally, crossing the threshold into a sanctuary of Jewish living. Tradition decrees that the mezuzah be affixed to the door within thirty days of moving in. The occasion can be made into a beautiful ceremony, perhaps part of the housewarming, thus immediately establishing the tone of the Jewish household.

It would be a good idea to have your rabbi, or an informed friend or relative, explain the significance of the mezuzah. In addition to the formal *berahah* (thanksgiving) a reading from the Psalms would be appropriate.

The mezuzah gives you your first opportunity to express the Jewish spirit artistically in your home. Both in the United States and in Israel silversmiths and other craftsmen are creating original and handsomely designed *mezuzot*. Some are of simple but excellent design, modest in price; others are magnificent in artistry and of priceless heirloom value. Fortunately, there is more than one door in a household, so that different kinds of *mezuzot* can be used. An original gift for a new baby might be a tiny mezuzah for the nursery or bedroom door.

BLESSING ON AFFIXING A MEZUZAH IN A NEW HOME

בָּרוּךְ אַתָּה יְיָ אֱלֹהֵינוּ מֶלֶךְ הָעוֹלָם, אֲשֶׁר קִדְּשָׁנוּ בְּמִצְוֹתָיו וְצִוָּנוּ לִקְבֹּעַ מְזוּזָה:

baruh atah adonai elohenu meleh ha'olam asher kideshanu bemitz-votav vetzivanu likbo'a mezuzah

Blessed art Thou, Lord our God, King of the universe, Who has sanctified us with Thy commandments, and instructed us to attach a mezuzah.

בָּרוּךְ אַתָּה יְיָ אֱלֹהֵינוּ מֶלֶךְ הָעוֹלָם, שֶׁהֶחֱיָנוּ וְקִיְּמָנוּ וְהִגִּיעָנוּ לַזְּמָן הַזֶּה:

baruh atah adonai elohenu meleh ha'olam sheheheyanu vekiye-manu vehigiyanu lazeman hazeh

Blessed art Thou, Lord our God, King of the universe, Who has kept us in life, preserved us, and enabled us to reach this season.

SOMETHING OLD, SOMETHING NEW

No MATTER WHETHER the décor of your home is "period" or modern, simple or elaborate, Jewish ceremonial objects are always in place. Today, these are available in either traditional or contemporary design. Young newlyweds should not overlook the value of family heirlooms or hand-me-downs.

START WITH THESE Just as important as your linens and dishes are these:

> Sabbath candlesticks
> Kiddush cup
> Hanukkah menorah
> Bible
> Prayer book

Through the years other important ceremonial objects may be purchased or received as gifts.

IN TIME For the Sabbath, you will be able to enhance your décor by using a special:

HALLAH TRAY. Many are made with wooden slicing boards in the center so that the loaves may be cut easily after the *motzi* (blessing over the bread) is recited.

HALLAH CLOTH. It could be home-designed and attractively embroidered or crocheted.

HALLAH KNIFE. Some have handles appropriately decorated.

WINE DECANTER. Also available are silver markers with the legend *"bore peri hagafen."*

SPICE-BOX *(besamim)*, *havdallah* tray and braided candle for the *havdallah* ceremony (page 70).

These articles will be used all year round—at least fifty-two times—so they should be bought with a feeling for beauty, dignity and importance.

Children enjoy participating in the kiddush when they have their own special little kiddush cups. There are many fitting occasions (the baby's birth, or perhaps a birthday or a holiday visit) for giving a child his own silver cup.

For the festivals, it is nice to have these:

PURIM. An illustrated megillah—the Book of Esther, written on a scroll.

SUKKOT. An *etrog* box of wood, silver, china, etc.

PESACH. A Seder plate with sections for the symbolic foods; a *matzot* cover; the Cup of Elijah; Haggadahs—beautifully printed and illustrated.

SOME HELPFUL HINTS A *magen david* (the term popularly applied to a six-pointed star) on a ceremonial object does not necessarily give it a true Jewish character. Some gift shops in catering to the desire for objects of Jewish interest are indiscriminate in their selections. Make your purchases carefully. See what your Sisterhood gift shop offers. If it doesn't have what you want, one of the chairmen will probably know where to get it. Many Jewish organizations have book and gift shops, and there are private dealers in large cities.

This is a good place to call your attention to the "Directory of Israel Products" published by the Office of the Israel Trade Commissioner in the United States and the American-Israel Chamber of Commerce and Industry, Inc. at 500 Fifth Avenue, New York, N. Y.

10110. This free pamphlet lists the products of Israel—from art and apparel to wishniak and wood—on sale in the United States, with a list of their importers and agents.

Visits to museums such as the Jewish Museum in New York City, and others in the list on page 12, and a glance at the books listed on page 13, will be helpful. The Jewish Museum has many special exhibits during the year to which members receive invitations.

THE FINE ART OF LIVING

THERE ARE MANY WAYS in which your home can develop a personality—through paintings, books and music. With the heightened interest in art today, original water colors, etchings, and even oil paintings are within the range of a modest budget. It is not unusual to come into a charmingly appointed living room and find, equally at home on the walls, a seascape of Maine, an abstract still life and a water color of Haifa.

This is not the place for a discussion of what constitutes Jewish art. Israeli artists and American artists interested in Jewish subjects, however, should be encouraged in their work. Watch for exhibitions of Israeli artists held from time to time in cities throughout the United States. Articles on this subject by art critics appear in newspapers and magazines occasionally.

The ingathering in Israel of Jews of many lands has resulted in a variety of creative artistic expressions which are meeting with great favor in the American market. In the craft field, there is no limit to the imagination of contemporary Jewish artisans—working with dolls, small tapestries, embroidered pictures of Biblical scenes, decorated tiles, modern and exotic costume jewelry. You can easily find beautiful wood carvings and ceramics of hassidim, halutzim, of Yemenite dancers.

Amateur photographers will find effective material in almost any holiday scene, such as a starry-eyed child kindling the Hanukkah lights. A tourist can bring back photographs of Jewish places of interest, like the Touro Synagogue in Newport, Rhode Island, or of a scene in Israel. Such photographs, properly enlarged, grouped and framed, add interest to a room.

There are old illuminated maps, maps of Biblical place names in the United States (see the end of this chapter) and picture maps of Jewish history. These maps are not only decorative, but serve as educational conversation pieces when framed and hung in the den or family room. Old Israeli coins and modern commemorative ones can be mounted on velvet and framed for the study or for a boy's room.

Indicating these various areas of decoration in no way suggests that a home should be restricted to Jewish objects of beauty; on the contrary, these will be effective only if they fit comfortably into the general atmosphere of the home, where they are wanted and appreciated.

ON THE SHELF In this age of paperbacks and digests, it is still important to have books of permanence and beauty in your home. Build a good family library. No Jewish home should be without these:

The Holy Scriptures—the Jewish Publication Society edition
   is a recommended one
Siddur—the daily and Sabbath prayer book
Mahzor—the Holy Day and Festival prayer book

Your bookshelves would be incomplete without some books of Jewish history, art, literature, music; various books suited to your special Jewish interest; books on holidays; books on Israel and Zionism.

The lists given at the end of each chapter and at the end of this book are not intended to be all-inclusive bibliographies. The suggestions are made with the hope of opening new vistas for you and your family.

There are books in the Jewish field for every age group. You can find play books for tots, do-it-yourself books for teenagers and recipe books for the homemaker. The publishers of exclusively Jewish material have comprehensive catalogs. (See page 12.) Some of the general trade publishers have special departments for books of Jewish interest.

The family might treat itself to membership in the Jewish Publication Society, 1930 Chestnut Street, Philadelphia, Pa. 19103 or the Jewish Book Guild of America, 11 East 36th Street, New York , N. Y. Subscription rates are modest. The books are of lasting value and interest. The Conservative, Orthodox and Reform groups all issue a number of excellent books. Your Sisterhood book and gift shops will be helpful in your book buying. They might also be featuring attractive bookplates, sometimes designed by Jewish artists.

PERIODICALLY GOOD   You probably receive some Anglo-Jewish periodicals through your various affiliations. In addition, you might like to subscribe to some others of Jewish cultural interest. The *American Jewish Yearbook,* published by the American Jewish Committee and the Jewish Publication Society, gives a fairly comprehensive listing. Examine the magazines and periodicals in your synagogue or center library to see which might interest you.

There are both Yiddish and English publications in many fields. *Hadoar,* the only non-technical Hebrew periodical in the United States, is worthy of support. For children, *World Over* is highly recommended. Published by the Board of Jewish Education, 426 West 58th Street, New York, N. Y. 10019, it is noted for its attractive format and lively content.

DAY BY DAY   While not in the same category as books or magazines, a Jewish calendar is an essential item in every home. A *lu'ah* provides you with the correct candlelighting time; it helps you plan your holidays; it will be a reminder of "yahrzeit" and other significant occasions. You can get a *lu'ah* (there are pocket and desk varieties) through your Sisterhood gift shop, from various national Jewish organizations, or by writing to one of the manufacturers of kosher foods or other products familiar to the Jewish housewife (see Chapter 6).

ON THE RECORD   Like all record-collectors today, the Jewish family finds a wide choice of special-interest material. There are regular and long-playing records of holiday music, cantorial and liturgical music, modern Israeli songs, children's songs and symphonies. Chapter 15 gives some specific listings. Consult also "Guides to Recordings," National Jewish Music Council, 15 East 26th Street, New York City.

A DOUBLE MITZVAH

THE EXPRESSION OF LOVE for God through the enjoyment of beautiful objects and good music is as old as Judaism itself. The earliest artistic expression in Jewish life, in the home or the synagogue, stems from the verse "This is my God and I will glorify Him"

(Exodus 15.2). In enriching and enhancing your home, you are performing a double mitzvah.

WHERE TO BUY CEREMONIAL OBJECTS, HOLIDAY ACCESSORIES AND BOOKS

Check your Sisterhood gift and book shops first; they may have what you want or can suggest where to get it. In New York and other large cities, a number of commercial shops and establishments sell religious articles, works of art, ceremonial objects, books, imports from Israel, games, records or other items of special Jewish interest.

The few listed here are run by organizations:

Women's League for Conservative Judaism
48 East 74 Street
New York, N. Y. 10021

United Synagogue Book Service
New York

Hadassah Book Order Service
New York

Zionist Organization of America Gift and Book Shop
New York

Union of Orthodox Jewish Congregations
New York

Union of American Hebrew Congregations Book Shop
New York

NOTE: The National Jewish Welfare Board has available a list of places where Jewish prints and works of art for the home may be bought.

MUSEUMS AND COLLECTIONS OF JUDAICA

The Jewish Museum
Fifth Avenue and 92nd Street
New York   N. Y.

Jewish Theological Seminary of America
Broadway and 122nd Street
New York   N. Y.

Hebrew Union College
Clifton Avenue
Cincinnati   Ohio

There is also a collection of Judaica at the Smithsonian Institution in Washington, D. C.

SOME PUBLISHERS IN THE JEWISH FIELD

Behrman House
New York

Bloch Publishing Company
New York

Hebrew Publishing Company
New York

Jewish Publication Society
Philadelphia

Jewish Reconstructionist Foundation
New York

Women's League for Conservative Judaism
New York

Schocken Books Inc.
New York

Union of American Hebrew Congregations
New York

United Synagogue of America
New York

NOTE: For reading lists, refer to the Jewish Book Council of America, 15 East 26th Street, New York City.

THESE BOOKS MIGHT BE USEFUL

❧ ON CEREMONIAL OBJECTS

ANCIENT HEBREW ARTS by A. Reifenberg (Schocken). Art relics of Jewish antiquity in more than 200 illustrations. Explanations relate the objects to Jewish history.

JEWISH CEREMONIAL ART by Stephen S. Kayser and Guido Schoenberger (Jewish Publication Society). Illustrated book and catalog of ceremonial objects, most of them from the Jewish Museum in New York City.

JEWISH CEREMONIAL OBJECTS by Philip Goodman (National Jewish Welfare Board). A pamphlet with descriptions and illustrations of ceremonial objects and articles on ceremonial art.

BAR MITZVAH by Abraham I. Katsh (Shengold Publishers). An anthology of stories and articles on religion, tradition and history. Makes a good Bar Mitzvah gift. Mentioned here because of its excellent photographs of ceremonial objects.

❧ ON ART

A HISTORY OF JEWISH ART by Franz Landsberger (Union of American Hebrew Congregations). A discussion of the art of the Jewish people in relation to its background and history; art in the synagogue and home; the development of Jewish art from its beginnings to 1946. Illustrated.

JEWISH ARTISTS OF THE 19TH AND 20TH CENTURIES by Karl Schwarz (Philosophical Library). Although this book was published in 1949, it is still valuable as a summary of the contributions of Jewish artists of the 19th and 20th centuries. Good reproductions.

THE JERUSALEM WINDOWS by Marc Chagall, notes by Jean Lemaire (Braziller). Superb color illustrations and two original unsigned color lithographs.

LOVE AND JOY ABOUT LETTERS by Ben Shahn (Grossman). Illustrations of lettering, mostly Hebrew—with texts from Jewish sources.

❧ ON MUSIC

MUSIC OF THE JEWS by Aron Mark Rothmueller (Thomas Yoseloff). A nontechnical historical survey of music that can be attributed to a recognized Jewish tradition. An intelligent presentation for the layman.

BOOKS AND ARTICLES ON JEWISH MUSIC by Joseph Yasser (National Jewish Music Council). A bibliography.

❧ YOU MIGHT LIKE TO OWN

GREAT JEWISH PORTRAITS IN METAL edited by Daniel M. Friedenberg. Introduction by Cecil Roth (Schocken, hardcover and paperback folio). Outstanding Jewish personalities depicted on medals and plaques, each with a concise biography.

LAND OF OUR FATHERS—a handsomely illustrated map in full color of Biblical place names in America created by Dr. Moshe Davis and Lottie Davis, illustrated by Charles Harper and published by the Associated American Artists Galleries, 711 Fifth Avenue, New York 22, N. Y. The map, unframed, measures 32¾ x 22½ inches and costs $3.95. An interesting booklet, "A Guide to Map of Biblical Names in America," is included with each map.

PAINTING IN ISRAEL—a portfolio with excellent reproductions in full color of a representative group of contemporary Israeli painters. Published by Mikra Studio in Israel, it is available here.

VIEWS OF THE BIBLICAL WORLD (International Publishing Co., Ltd., Ramat Gan, Israel). The first of four volumes depicting the physical, ethnic, and historical background of the Bible. Vivid full-color photographs, handsome format, Biblical text and commentary.

CHAPTER 2

Occupation: Housewife

"She looketh well to the ways of her household"
(Proverbs 31:27)

2

Occupation: Housewife

L IFE IN THE SMALL TOWN in the old country was simple. The Jewish housewife in her kitchen faced hard work but few complications. Everybody observed kashrut. Poultry was taken to the local shohet. It never occurred to a housewife to buy non-kosher meat. The question of "milchig" or "fleishig" cooking was simple; shortening was either butter for dairy, chicken fat for meat dishes, or oil for "pareve." There were no packaged or frozen foods to complicate choices. On any question, the local rabbi was the final authority.

On the other hand, while life today is generally more complex, kashrut for the Jewish housewife is made easier by scientific aids and government supervision. For example, all processed foods must be labeled and the ingredients clearly identified. More and more, vegetable fats are being used in prepared foods. Kosher meat products must undergo government inspection as well as rabbinical supervision.

FOOD FOR THOUGHT—WHY THE DIETARY LAWS?

MANY REASONS ARE ADVANCED for observing the dietary rules of Judaism. Traditionalists believe that these laws are divinely ordained to help keep us a holy people. Others add that they are hygienically wise. There are those who stress the spiritual value of the discipline involved, while some modernists maintain that these laws should be observed in order to perpetuate Jewish identity.

However, all these would no doubt agree that the laws of kashrut have been a significant factor in forming the unique character of the Jewish home. By means of these rules, religion enters the kitchen and accompanies the family to the table. Let us bear in mind that these laws are concerned basically with the taking of animal life to provide food for human beings. The avoidance of predatory birds and beasts of prey; the absolute prohibition of all blood; the limitation of meat to the flesh of a few grass-eating species, carefully slaughtered under religious supervision by a method designed to avoid unnecessary pain; all these are reminders of a deep reverence for life, of a humane and sensitive ethic.

In the traditional Jewish home, the preparation of a nutritious, tasteful and attractive meal is desirable, but that is not enough. Through the observance of kashrut, your preparation of foods and your daily household chores are raised above their utilitarian purposes.

WHAT DOES "KOSHER" MEAN? The root of the Hebrew word kosher means "properly prepared." In connection with food, it has come to mean "ritually proper." Its opposite is *tref* (feminine: *trefah*), a word which originally meant "torn by a beast of prey," and now means simply "non-kosher."

We want to be perfectly clear about the meaning of these words, so that you will not be misled by the phrase "kosher-style," a contradiction in terms often used in the advertising of hotels and restaurants that seek a Jewish clientele. It is also misused on the labels and advertising for some commercial foods and beverages.

The word kosher does *not* describe a kind of menu, cuisine or style of cooking. You can make kosher ravioli, shish kebab, madrilene or crêpes suzette. On the other hand, you can get "gefillte" fish, "k'naidlach," "tzimmes," and other so-called Jewish dishes which might be quite *tref*. They would be, unless any animal substance they contained were: 1) from a kosher species, 2) properly prepared, 3) not combined in a non-kosher mixture.

ANIMAL, VEGETABLE, MINERAL   First, let us set aside the vegetable and mineral kingdoms, to which the laws of kashrut do
not apply. (It may be interesting to recall that the Torah describes
the first, unspoiled human beings in the garden of Eden as vege-
tarians.) There are no prohibited vegetable or mineral foods. Such
foods are neutral as far as mixtures with milk or meat foods are
concerned.

Then, we turn our attention to the animal kingdom—the fishes,
the birds, and the beasts. Which species are kosher?

Let us start with the fishes, lowest in the evolutionary scale.
"These may ye eat of all that are in the waters: whatsoever hath
fins and scales . . ," (Leviticus 11:9). The term "fish" is used to
include all water creatures, so that shellfish, frogs, whale and the
like are prohibited. To qualify, fish must have fins and scales in
their natural state. No special preparation is necessary; no problems of mixture arise. This takes care of the fish.

But for warm-blooded creatures—animals and fowl—the situation is different. Proceeding up the scale, we ask: what species of
birds are kosher? According to the Torah, all birds except the
twenty-four kinds mentioned in Leviticus 11:13-19. These are ap-
parently birds of prey, such as the eagle, vulture, raven, owl, and
hawk. No physical qualifications are given, although the Talmud
does supply some complicated ones; these, however, need not
concern the housewife. If she wants a kosher bird, she must have
one that has been ritually slaughtered, so that the selection of
the species has already been made by an expert. A sample list of
permitted and prohibited foods appears on the next two pages.

As for animals, the Torah is explicit. "Whatsoever parteth the
hoof, and is wholly cloven-footed, and cheweth the cud, among
the beasts, that may ye eat" (Leviticus 11:3). That limits us to a
few grasseaters—the cow, the sheep, the goat. The deer and its
cousins qualify, but kosher venison is hard to come by, because it
would mean that a healthy specimen would have to be caught
unharmed and then ritually slaughtered.

KOSHER PREPARATION   For birds and animals, as you already
know, it is not enough that they belong to the right species. To
become kosher meat or fowl, they must (1) be properly slaughtered; (2) be examined to eliminate diseased animals; (3) have

Fish

Anchovies
Bass
Bluefish
Butterfish
Carp
Caviar (roe of kosher fish)
Cod
Flounder
Fluke
Haddock
Halibut
Herring
Mackerel
Pike
Porgy
Red Snapper
Salmon
Sardines
Shad
Smelt
Sole
Sturgeon (kosher varieties)
Trout
Tuna
Weakfish
Whitefish

Fowl

Capon
Chicken
Domestic Dove
Domestic Duck
Domestic Goose
Domestic Pigeon (squab)
Domestic Turkey

Meat

Cow (calf, beef, veal)
Goat
Lamb

Sea Food

Clams
Crab
Eel
Frogs
Lizard
Lobster
Octopus
Oysters
Scallops
Shrimp
Snails
Turtle

Fowl

Wild Duck
Wild Goose
Wild Turkey
Any other game birds

Meat

Game
Pig (pork, ham, bacon, etc.)

(These are not comprehensive lists,
merely samplings. On any questions
and for further information,
consult your rabbi.)

forbidden parts, such as certain hindquarters, removed; (4) be free of blood.

The first three of these steps are taken care of for you by the shohet. He is a highly trained man, certified as a scholar in the laws of kashrut, an expert in the practice of *shehita*, and a person of upright character. Before taking the life of bird or beast, he must pronounce a prayer. It is well to know that such sensitivity underlies the Jewish dietary laws.

As for the fourth step in the preparation—the elimination of prohibited blood—this, too, is nowadays made easy for the homemaker. On request, many reliable butchers will take care of this process, popularly called "koshering." The market today offers frozen meats and fowl which have been prepared completely according to the requirements of kashrut. Nevertheless, such services may not always be available. The basic procedure for koshering meat and fowl at home is therefore given here.

KOSHERING MEAT AT HOME

1. Soak the meat in cold water for half an hour in a special utensil set aside for this purpose; drain and rinse.

2. Sprinkle with salt on all sides and in all folds; place for one hour upon a slanted board, preferably perforated, which allows the blood to drain off.

3. Wash the meat under cold running water.

It is now ready for cooking.

NOTE: Meat for broiling need not be koshered as above. Simply wash surface blood off, sprinkle with salt, and then proceed to broil. The blood which drains off is not kosher.

Liver is never koshered with other meat. It is scored in two directions, washed, and broiled over an open flame. Then it may be fried, sautéed or prepared in any other way. When cooking is done on an electric stove, the liver must be rotated during the process of broiling and the blood drained off.

KOSHERING FOWL

1. Remove all organs from the center cavity.

2. If the feet are to be used, remove the claws and skin.

3. Proceed as for koshering meat.

MILK AND MEAT   You probably remember that there is a third requirement for kosher meat. In addition to being of the right species, properly prepared, it must not be mixed with milk, or with milk products. Three times the Torah repeats the law "thou shalt not seethe a kid in its mother's milk." From this Biblical injunction the whole practice of separation of milk products from meat products arises. One reason given for the prohibition is that the kid cooked in its mother's milk was used in ancient idolatrous rites. A revulsion against the inhumanity of this act is also cited as a reason. To quote from a distinguished Christian scholar: "We no longer know by what revolting sight this prohibition may have been called forth, but evidently that phrase became a kind of memorial by which Israel should always be reminded of that considerate humanity which was to distinguish it from the barbarous nations."

This system of separation means that no meat or foods containing meat or its derivatives should be prepared, cooked, served or eaten with milk or foods containing milk or its derivatives.

The terms often used to distinguish the two kinds of food are "milchig" (milk) and "fleishig" (meat). After eating a "fleishig" meal, one is not supposed to eat "milchig" foods until a certain time has elapsed—from one to six hours, depending on varying local custom. Food which is neither milk nor meat is often called "pareve" (neutral) and may be eaten at any time or with any meal.

PAREVE FOODS You will be glad to be reminded that all vegetables and purely vegetable or mineral products are "pareve," and don't have to be separated from anything.

Fish which needs no *shehitah* or koshering is also "pareve."

And so are eggs. But there are some points to remember about eggs. An egg, with or without shell, that is found in poultry, is "fleishig." It must be treated the same way as the rest of the fowl.

And another point about "the egg and you." If an egg, on being opened, is found to have a speck of blood on it, it is *tref* and must be discarded. The speck indicates that the process of fertilization, which is to say life, has already begun.

WHAT'S IN A LABEL?

IN THE STORES TODAY there is a constantly expanding list of kosher foods, packaged or canned or frozen, partially or completely prepared. These include delicatessen products and frozen foods like "blintzes" and "kreplach" which need only to be heated before serving. Manufacturers are trying to be more vigilant in engaging accredited rabbis to supervise departments for the preparation of modern kosher food products.

Those manufacturers who are eager to serve the Jewish consumer use the identification mark Ⓤ on products authorized by rabbinical authority. The Ⓤ signifies Union of Orthodox Jewish Congregations and items with this label are immediately recognized as kosher. This does not imply that there are not valid endorsements by other competent agencies or individual rabbis; where there is a question, check with your local rabbi.

BREAD-AND-BUTTER   Bread may contain milk or non-kosher ingredients even though these are not listed on the package. There are enough breads on the market clearly listing their ingredients so there need be no doubt which to buy.

There are many vegetable shortenings on the market.

In buying margarine, remember that even vegetable margarine is not necessarily "pareve," since milk may be used in its manufacture. There are, however, "pareve" margarines that may be used for "milchig" or "fleishig."

JUST DESSERTS   Science has come to the aid of the modern Jewish cook! You now can buy a synthetic topping made from soybeans which tastes and looks just like cream. There are also flavored and unflavored kosher gelatin substitutes prepared without an animal base. Both of these make possible an unlimited variety of attractive and delicious molds, mousses, ices, sherbets and other desserts for both meat and dairy meals.

SEPARATE DISHES

SEPARATION OF MEAT AND MILK PRODUCTS means that the kosher home has to have separate sets of dishes, kitchen utensils, silverware and dish towels for "milchig" and "fleishig." These must be washed in separate dishpans and stored in separate areas. While this may seem involved for you, it is actually simple once the home is set up for it. In purchasing china, silver and other items, select different designs for the milk and meat sets to make them easily distinguishable. Choose towels in different color schemes or patterns.

You might also include in your kitchen extra dishes made of glass. Since glass is nonabsorbent, such dishes are "pareve" and may be used for either dairy or meat. For example, these might be used for fruit served at a dairy meal, and again for fruit served at a meat meal. It is not advisable to use one set of glass dishes for all purposes. Such a practice could easily lead to an eventual abolition of any distinction between meat and dairy.

PASSOVER DISHES The kosher home will also have two sets of dishes, utensils and the like, exclusively for Passover use since no *ḥametz* (leaven) may come into contact with dishes used for this season. But that is a different subject and will be explained in Chapter 8. Refer to that section before purchasing or providing dishes for Passover.

UTENSILS AND EQUIPMENT

1. *An electric dishwasher* may be used for both meat and dairy dishes provided separate trays are used—one for meat and one for dairy. Meat and dairy dishes, obviously, should not be washed at the same time.

2. *One electric mixer or blender* may be used if there are separate bowls and blenders for "milchig" and "fleishig."

3. *One electric broiler* with separate trays for milk and meat foods may be used. Covering the tray with fresh aluminum foil for each use is an alternative method of separation.

4. *In the freezer* it is easy and efficient to arrange separate sections for milk and meat foods. All meat should be koshered before freezing.

There are many well-known detergents and synthetic soaps which are acceptable without specific endorsement if none of the ingredients contain animal substances.

A PLACE FOR EVERYTHING Where there is ample cabinet space, it is easy for you to arrange separate cabinets for "milchig" and "fleishig" dishes and utensils. But even in the small compact kitchen, separate shelves can be set aside for the two kinds of dishes. You will find this easy if you make it part of your basic planning for your kosher kitchen. Labels and lists indicating "milchig" and "fleishig" identify cabinets or shelves for visitors or household help. Variations in color schemes and patterns of dishes, utensils and linens make for quick recognition.

THE WAY OF A MAID If you have a maid or other household help, give her clear, simple directions concerning the separation of milk and meat foods, dishes, utensils and linens. A general information list should be attached inside a cabinet door where it can readily be seen. This is a good time to remind you that no heavy chores should be done by the maid or other help on the Sabbath or Festivals.

THE BUSINESS OF BEING
A "BALABOSTEH"

THE HOMEY YIDDISH EXPRESSION "BALABOSTEH" literally means "mistress of the home," from the Hebrew *ba'alat habayit*. The significance of this phrase, suggesting an important executive, should offset the diffidence we sometimes feel when we fill out a form "Occupation—Housewife," and should raise our status in our own eyes. The management of a home in the Jewish tradition is a dignified, important and rewarding job.

HOUSEHOLD HINTS

Caution: Hebrew lettering on a store or a product does not necessarily indicate kashrut. Signs can be misleading; for example, בשר בשר which means merely "Meat Meat," glanced at quickly might be mistaken for בשר כשר which means "Kosher Meat."

Kosher meals, endorsed by the Union of Orthodox Jewish Congregations of America, are now obtainable on request on some airlines and ocean liners, as well as in certain hospitals. Indicate that you want kosher meals when you buy your ticket or enter a hospital.

New food imports from Israel are now available in major department stores and supermarkets.

Into the mouths of babes: kosher baby foods containing meat and combinations of meat and vegetables are now available, so that both feeding at home and traveling with an infant are considerably simplified.

Send for the Kosher Products Directory, published annually by the Kashruth Division, Union of Orthodox Jewish Congregations of America, 116 East 27th Street, New York, N. Y. 10016. The Union also publishes a monthly *News Reporter* which gives information on newly certified kosher products. A postcard will place you on its mailing list—there is no charge.

THESE ARE GOOD FOR REFERENCE

THE JEWISH DIETARY LAWS, THEIR MEANING FOR OUR TIME—by Rabbi Samuel H. Dresner (National Academy of Adult Jewish Studies of the United Synagogue of America).

CHAPTER 3

From Cradle to Canopy

"There are three partners in the molding of every human being—God, his father, and his mother" (Talmud)

3

From Cradle to Canopy

HAVING A BABY not only increases your size temporarily; it broadens your horizons permanently. In the months of waiting, you will have time to think and many things to think about—the extra room, the kind of crib, the layette; whether the baby will be a girl or a boy and what to name "it."

WHAT'S IN A NAME?

CAREFUL THOUGHT SHOULD BE GIVEN to the choice of a name for the new baby. For Jewish parents, the question has two aspects. Baby should be given a Hebrew name, and consideration must be given to its equivalent in English. Several factors will govern the choice —family sentiment, individual taste, meaning, historical association, and—let's face it—current fashion. It can seem very confusing, but don't let it get you down.

THE HEBREW NAME Every Jewish boy or girl should be given a name in Hebrew. It is one of the oldest—and most persistent—forms of Jewish identification. Besides, the Hebrew name will be needed later on, for being called to the Torah, for use in Hebrew school, for inscription on the religious school diploma and other documents, and for inclusion in the *ketubah* (marriage certificate). When the child is old enough, he or she should be told this Hebrew name, along with the father's, because Jewish tradition uses the old Biblical style—Joseph *ben* (son of) David, or Sarah *bat* (daughter of) Reuben. (Family names are a later development among all peoples; with Jews, they are nearly all of comparatively recent vintage.)

The custom of naming a child for a member of the family no longer living is neither universal nor obligatory; it is not at all prescribed by Jewish law. Nevertheless, it is a tradition which helps to preserve the memory of a dear one. The immediate situation of your own family will help you decide whether to adhere to this practice.

You may run into some difficulty in trying to name a child after a relative of the opposite sex. Only a few Hebrew names are easily adaptable, such as Simhah (Joy), which can be used for either boy or girl; or Nahum (Comfort) for the masculine and Nehamah for the feminine form. More often than not, you will have to look for a name with an allied meaning, or even merely a similar sound. Better still, why not reserve the desired name for your next and hope it will be a girl (or boy).

There is a strong feeling among most Jews against naming a child after a living parent, either in Hebrew or in English.

THE ENGLISH NAME   Most of the classical Hebrew names are at home in the English language in forms equally historic and rich in association, especially when they come from the Bible. There is no need to look for so-called modern "equivalents," such as Stanley for Samuel, or Rhoda for Rebecca, where the only resemblance is the first letter of the name. Happily, there is a revival today of the strong, colorful Biblical names that are part of America's Puritan tradition—Jonathan, Benjamin, David, Elihu, Sarah, Rebecca, Rachel, Leah, Miriam, Daniel, Deborah, Michael, and many more.

To be sure, you may not readily find an English version of the Hebrew name you have chosen. Don't give up. There may be a derived form. Elizabeth, Anne, Jeremy, Zachary, Martha, and Matthew are all of Hebrew origin. Or you may follow the principle of meaning: Malcah means the same as Regina (queen); Aryeh means Lion or Leo; Baruch (blessed) means the same as Benedict. Finally, and as a last resort, there is the principle of similar sound, referred to above.

On all these questions, as well as for suggestions about naming a child after a great personality, or using a combination of names, you may find it useful to consult *These Are the Names* by Alfred Kolatch, published by Jonathan David, New York.

A WORD OF CAUTION   In your eagerness to give the baby a distinctive name, don't burden him with one so exotic or unconventional that it will make him uncomfortable when he grows up. And don't choose a name obviously out of place. Christopher and Christine are very nice, but plainly inappropriate for a Jewish child.

IF IT'S A GIRL

WHEN A BABY IS BORN, if it's a girl, the father should notify the synagogue officials of her arrival and of his plans to have her named at a service. Though the baby is not brought there, she is named in the synagogue during the reading of the Torah on the Sabbath or the Monday or Thursday (Torah reading days) immediately following her birth. Sometimes the date is postponed so that the mother can be present.

The father is honored with an aliyah (called up to the Torah) and the name is announced in the prayer, the *mi sheberah*, offered for the well-being of the mother and child.

IF IT'S A BOY

THE FATHER IS USUALLY CALLED to the Torah on the Sabbath following the birth of a boy, too, and may offer the prayer for his wife and son. But the boy is not named then; that is reserved for the eighth day of the boy's life, when a special ceremony takes place—the *brit milah* or covenant of circumcision.

"This is My covenant . . . every male among you shall be circumcised. . . . And he that is eight days old shall be circumcised among you, every male throughout your generations. . . ." (Genesis 17.10 and 12.)

This minor surgical operation is recommended by physicians today on a purely hygienic basis and is now practiced among most non-Jews. This religious service, however, requires a *mohel*, a Jew of piety highly qualified by training and experience for this task. The question often arises—why can't the circumcision be performed by a doctor instead of the *mohel?* The answer is that, for the Jew, this is not merely surgery, it is a religious ceremony. It is the sign of God's covenant "sealed into the very flesh of the child." For a similar reason, the eighth day is adhered to strictly, even though it be a Sabbath or Festival.

Whenever possible, the *brit* should be performed in the presence of a minyan (a religious quorum of ten males over the age of thirteen). The father and the *mohel* are counted as part of the minyan. Circumcision takes place on the eighth day, however, even when there is no minyan present.

It is considered a high honor to assist in this ceremony. The *sandek* is the person who holds the child during the circumcision; the "kvatter" and "kvatterin" (godparents) carry the infant from the mother to the *sandek*. The wish is expressed that the baby boy will grow up to *"Torah, ḥuppah, ma'asim tovim,"* to a long life marked by knowledge of the Torah, a happy marriage and good deeds.

Circumcision may be postponed only on the insistence of the physician, in consultation with the rabbi, for the protection of the child's health.

The circumcision ceremony is an occasion for family celebration, which may take place right in the hospital where special rooms are provided. Most hospitals in large cities accredit one *mohel* or more to their staffs. It would be wise to consult the hospital's regulations in advance to be sure that the *mohel* will be permitted to perform the *brit*, that rooms will be available, and to learn how many guests may be accommodated.

In more recent years, the circumcision often takes place at home, since mothers frequently leave the hospital after four or five days. The festivities and refreshments should be simple, out of consideration for the mother.

PIDYON HABEN   When the first-born child is a son, a special ceremony takes place on the thirty-first day after birth. This ceremony, evoking memories of ancient days, is called *pidyon haben* (redemption of the son). It is wise to consult your rabbi before planning this event, because there are various qualifications and limitations.

The Bible commands, "sanctify unto Me all the first-born" (Exodus 13.1). This was interpreted to mean that a father was either to dedicate his first-born son to the service of the Holy Temple or to redeem him by paying five shekels (approximately five dollars) to a *kohen* (one of priestly lineage). This ceremony does not apply when either the father or the mother is of a priestly or Levitic family.

For this occasion, a *kohen* is specially invited to the home. The baby is brought in on a cushion and, in the presence of the assembled family and friends, placed on a table. Five silver dollars are laid beside him. These can be obtained at a bank. Later, the *kohen* usually gives the "redemption money" to a worthy project.

In the presence of those assembled, an ancient dialogue takes place between the father and the *kohen*. It is to be found in most prayer books. Some versions include additional English readings and provide for participation by the mother.

If a rabbi is present, ask him to explain the ceremony. The service may be concluded with blessings over wine and hallah, followed by refreshments.

THE ADOPTED CHILD

THE INFANT BROUGHT HOME FOR ADOPTION receives a joyous welcome. The baby girl is named in the synagogue; the baby boy is circumcised at the appropriate time. An adopted boy more than eight days old who has not already been circumcised should undergo this surgery as soon as legally and medically permissible. If he has been circumcised, but without a religious service, he should be initiated into the community of Israel as soon as possible. Consult your rabbi about this.

ANNOUNCEMENTS

IT'S FUN TO BE CLEVER and original in your announcements, but good taste is essential. Don't be flippant or take your tone from advertising commercials. The examples shown may suggest other appropriate ideas to you.

The announcement of the arrival of an adopted baby may present special problems. Notice the restrained phrasing in the example shown.

Mr. and Mrs. David Eli Green

joyfully announce the arrival of

Ruth Amy

born June 24, 1960

Come and see us soon

at

3406 Rosewood Lane

Susan, David and Ruth Amy

An adoption announcement, tactfully handled

"‏ורחל היתה יפת־תאר ויפת מראה„

*". . . and Rachel was of beautiful form
and fair to look upon"*

Clare and Hart Rotenberg

*are happy to announce
the birth of*

Rachel Leah

on Sunday, May 11th, 1958

An unusual birth announcement, with Biblical quotation

מִי שֶׁבֵּרַך

MAY HE, Who blessed our mothers Sarah, Rebekah, Rachel and Leah, bless her who has given birth, together with her daughter, born in a happy hour. Let her name be called in Israel
_____ bat _____
May her parents have the merit of leading her to the Torah, to the wedding canopy, and to good deeds. And let us say AMEN.

An attractive card for a baby girl; can be ordered from Women's League

WHAT TO GIVE?

SWEATERS, RATTLES, AND BOTTLE WARMERS are all useful gifts, but sometimes the baby gets more of these than he needs. A kiddush cup, a mezuzah for the baby's room, a Bible, *Our Baby* (a record book for baby's first five years, published by the Women's League), are all useful, meaningful, and can be kept for a lifetime. Contributions to the Torah fund; a tree planted in Israel; gifts to a synagogue or a community project; a United States or Israel Bond—all are gifts that will be appreciated.

Brit Milah   ברית עילה

A Son Enters the Covenant

May his name be called in Israel

ben

Baby was circumcised and named

On   Hebrew date   English date

Place

Mohel

Sandek

Kvator

Kvatorin

Guests

Comments

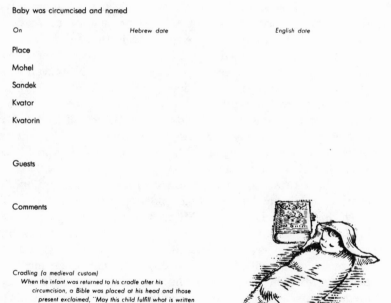

Cradling (a medieval custom)
   When the infant was returned to his cradle after his
     circumcision, a Bible was placed at his head and those
     present exclaimed, "May this child fulfill what is written
     in this Book."

An appropriate card for a baby boy; can be ordered from
Women's League

GROWING UP

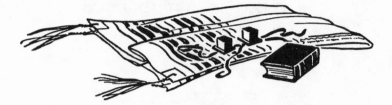

BAR MITZVAH

WHEN A BOY BECOMES THIRTEEN, he is given the opportunity to declare his loyalty to his people, to stand and be counted as a member of the household of Jewry. Henceforth, he dons his tefillin (phylacteries), is included in a minyan and as one of three males in a *mezuman* for the recital of grace. He is Bar Mitzvah (a son of the commandment) on this day and forever after.

The party, the presents, the festivities on this occasion are welcome, but they are really incidental to the significance of the ceremony. When a boy is called to the Torah as a Bar Mitzvah, he indicates his conscious acceptance of responsibility in his personal, family and religious life.

On this day he does not, contrary to popular conception, "become a man"; but he does take one step toward maturity. Too often, unfortunately, his Bar Mitzvah means a stopping-point in his Jewish studies. In many cases, the boy graduates from Hebrew school the same year. He should be encouraged to go on to a Hebrew high school, if one is available. If not, there may be a post-Bar Mitzvah class or club in your community. Where these are lacking, why not take the initiative of getting them organized? From this point on, more emphasis, not less, should be given to the boy's religious education.

Just what your son will do at the synagogue service when he celebrates his Bar Mitzvah will depend on the degree of Hebrew education he has received, and on the rules and regulations of your particular community. Many synagogues invite the boy and his parents to participate in the late Friday evening services preceding the morning that he is called to the Torah. He is often privileged to recite the kiddush or read an appropriate prayer. On the Sabbath of his Bar Mitzvah, he is called to the Torah for the reading of the maftir (the last portion of the weekly Torah reading). Often, if he is well prepared, he may even be asked to read the *sidrah* (portion of the week). Usually, he chants the Haftarah—the weekly Scripture lesson from the Prophets. Many congregations limit the privilege of reciting the Haftarah at Sabbath services to those boys who have received a certain minimum of Hebrew schooling. In some communities the requirement is five years. It is wise to learn the rules of your congregation while your children are still very young.

TEFILLIN Long before the important day, the Bar Mitzvah boy will get complete training and instruction from his father, his rabbi and his teachers. The mother and other members of his family should become familiar with his new morning routine—morning prayers in tefillin.

These are two small square boxes containing the parchment upon which four paragraphs from the Torah are inscribed. The tefillin, which the boy puts on daily except Sabbaths and Festivals, are bound with leather straps on the forehead (suggesting the mind) and on the left arm (near the heart).

Analogous to the "sign upon the doorpost" described in connection with the mezuzah (see page 3), these are "the sign upon the hand" and "the frontlets between thine eyes." Indeed, two of the paragraphs are the same as those in the mezuzah. The other two, which also contain these phrases, are from the book of Exodus, chapter 13, verses 1 to 10 and 11 to 16.

When your son winds the little leather thong around his finger, he recites: "And I will betroth thee unto Me forever; . . . in righteousness, and in justice, and in loving kindness and in compassion. And I will betroth thee unto Me in faithfulness, and thou shalt know the Lord" (Hosea 2:21-22).

In order that this become a relaxed, pleasant habit for the boy, the mother should see that he has ample time in the morning. The father, by example or appreciative recognition, can encourage him.

TALLIT The boy no doubt will have acquired a brand new *tallit* for his Bar Mitzvah. The *tallit* is the outer garment worn during morning prayers: "Speak unto the children of Israel, and bid them that they make throughout their generations fringes in the corners of their garments" (Numbers 15:38). These fringes are called *tzitzit*.

BAT MITZVAH

THE DAUGHTERS OF A JEWISH FAMILY, too, may mark their growing-up with a significant ceremony. Since girls mature earlier than boys, they are prepared for Bat Mitzvah (daughter of the commandment) any time after their twelfth birthday. This adolescent period requires understanding and patience on the part of the mother. Your daughter's Bat Mitzvah is a good time to encourage her homemaking skills and interests.

Although the status of Bat Mitzvah is an ancient and honored one, there has been no traditional ritual handed down in recognition of this step toward religious maturity. In recent years, however, many synagogues in America and to some extent in Israel have introduced varying types of ceremony for this occasion, in recognition of the increasing role of Jewish women in public life.

In most instances, the ceremony for girls has not been made a carbon copy of the Bar Mitzvah, though it frequently includes some of the same elements, such as the reading by the girl of a selection from the Prophets. As often as not, the Bat Mitzvah is celebrated at the Friday evening service; in some Orthodox synagogues, it is held on Sunday afternoon. Your local rabbi will, of course, determine what form the Bat Mitzvah ceremony will take.

CONFIRMATION

CONFIRMATION MAY BE ANOTHER HIGHLIGHT in your child's life. This is a group ceremony marking a completion of a specific period of Jewish study. The children are usually from fourteen to sixteen years of age, depending on local practice.

CELEBRATIONS   All these milestones—Bar Mitzvah, Bat Mitzvah and Confirmation—call for celebrations. Unfortunately, the joyous spirit of these events sometimes tends to obscure their religious nature. There has been undue emphasis, in some circles, on elaborate dances and cocktail parties completely inappropriate for the occasion and for the age of the boy or girl,

INVITATIONS The invitations should be simple but dignified and should emphasize the service. The examples shown here are appropriate to the beauty and spirit of the occasion.

Mr. & Mrs. Charles Stockler

request the pleasure of your company

on the occasion of the Barmitzvah

of their son

William Thomas

who will read Maftir and Haftorah

at the St. Johns Wood Synagogue

Abbey Road, N.W.8

on

Saturday 8th February 1958

at 10. a. m.

Reception
Buffet Luncheon
after the Service at
46, Springfield Road
N.W.8.   *R.S.V.P.*

A formal Bar Mitzvah invitation; synagogue in London, England

MR. AND MRS. HARVEY GOLDEN
invite you to participate in the
Sabbath Morning Services
at the Shaar Hashomayim Synagogue
on April twenty-sixth
nineteen hundred and fifty-two
at nine-thirty o'clock
when their son Alan Zebulon
will be called to the Torah
as a Bar-Mitzvah.

Reception at eight o'clock
Community Hall
Kensington Avenue

A formal engraved Bar Mitzvah invitation, giving
emphasis to the service

Rabbi and Mrs. Bernard Segal
invite you to participate in services
at the synagogue of the Jewish
Theological Seminary of America,
3080 Broadway, New York City,
on Thursday morning. March tenth,
nineteen hundred and fifty-five, at nine
o'clock, when their son, David will be
called to the Torah, on the occasion
of his Bar Mitzvah.

ב״ה

הרב ברוך הלוי סגל ורעיתו
חסידה מתכבדים להזמינכם
לתפלה בבית הכנסת של בית
המדרש לרבנים בניו־יורק
ביום ה׳ פרשת פרה תשט״ו
בשעה תשע בבקר ולהשתתף
בשמחתם בעלות בנם מרדכי
דוד לתורה ובהגיעו למצוות

An attractive Bar Mitzvah invitation. Interesting note—this Bar Mitzvah
took place on a *Thursday* morning

בס״ד

הרב שמואל גרשון כ״לוי
ורעיתו שושנה מתכבדים
להזמינכם לתפלה בשבת
פ' במדבר תש״ט בשעה.
תשע׳ בבקר ולדהשתתף
בשמחתם ביום שיעלד.
בנם דן שמעון לתורה
ויגיע למצוות

RABBI AND MRS. SAMUEL GERSHON LEVI
INVITE YOU TO PARTICIPATE IN
SABBATH SERVICES AT THE JAMAICA
JEWISH CENTER, ON MAY THE
TWENTY-EIGHTH, NINETEEN
HUNDRED AND FORTY-NINE, AT
NINE O'CLOCK, WHEN THEIR SON,
DON SIMEON, WILL BE CALLED TO
THE TORAH AS A BAR MITZVAH;
AND TO JOIN THEM AFTERWARDS
FOR KIDDUSH

A Bar Mitzvah announcement with Hebrew Torah script

Dr. and Mrs. Lawrence G. Kaplan
invite you to worship with
them at the Sabbath eve service
at the Jamaica Jewish Center,
Friday, the twenty fourth of April,
nineteen hundred and sixty four
at eight o'clock, when their
daughter Elizabeth Jane will
chant a portion of the Haftorah
on the occasion of her Bat
Mitzvah; and to join them at the
Oneg Shabbat after the service.

רני ושמחי בת־ציון
Sing and rejoice, O daughter of Zion…
Zechariah II, 14

A Bat Mitzvah invitation

בן עזאי אומר
חייב אדם ללמד
את בתו תורה

(Ben Asai says, "It is incumbent upon man to teach his daughter Torah.")

MR. AND MRS. DANIEL MOSES
INVITE YOU TO WORSHIP WITH THEM AT
THE HILLTOP JEWISH CENTER ON SABBATH
MORNING, MAY THIRD, NINETEEN HUNDRED
AND FIFTY-NINE, AND TO JOIN THEM AFTER-
WARDS FOR KIDDUSH IN CELEBRATION OF
THE BAT MITZVAH OF THEIR DAUGHTER,
SARA MICHAL

A handsome Bat Mitzvah invitation with Hebrew quotation

GIFTS　Most synagogues give the boy or girl a Bible or a prayer book. In any case, the family should see to it that those are among the gifts. A kiddush cup, a Purim megillah, a handsome *tallit* bag, a beautiful Haggadah, books and records of Jewish interest—are all appropriate gifts.

Almost any child would like to receive a watch (a reminder to make the best use of time), a camera, a chess set, or a stamp collector's album (including Israel stamps). A *tallit* clasp, an Israel anniversary coin made into a medallion or paperweight, Israeli art objects or jewelry, a subscription to a magazine in a Jewish field or membership in a Jewish book club are also suitable presents. Where it is feasible financially and practically, a trip to Israel is a memorable Bar Mitzvah or Bat Mitzvah gift.

DO discuss the Bar Mitzvah or Bat Mitzvah plans with your son or daughter and with the rabbi and Hebrew School principal.

Arrange the date with your synagogue at least ten months ahead..

Invite the rabbi, the president of the synagogue and of the Sisterhood, and the child's Hebrew school principal and teacher to the reception.

Invite the child's friends.

Make arrangements in advance with the synagogue about who should be called to the Torah.

Arrange with the synagogue about flowers for the pulpit.

Have your son or daughter give a gift in honor of the event to the junior congregation or to some institution of his choice; if possible, from his own savings.

Arrange a party for your child's Hebrew school classmates—perhaps right in the classroom.

Advise the guests not to bring infants or very young children to the services.

Advise friends not to bring gifts to the synagogue.

Dress appropriately.

Arrive on time for services.

Help maintain the dignity and sanctity of the service.

Join in the reading of prayers and in congregational singing.

Invite the congregation for kiddush after the services. Serve simple refreshments.

Ask the Bar Mitzvah to recite the kiddush and the *motzi* at the beginning of the meal.

Make your party, if you have one, simple—a lunch or dinner or an "at home" for family and friends.

Keep the decorations and menu simple and appropriate.

DON'T visit or exchange greetings during the services.

Don't let incidentals like souvenir match books, elaborate favors or fancy fanfare exhaust your energy, money and good humor and lessen the dignity of the occasion.

Don't try to outdo your neighbor.

MAZAL TOV

HERE COMES THE BRIDE

PREPARATION FOR A WEDDING is a joyous task but a wearing one. The date must be fixed, the invitations and flowers ordered, the menu and music planned. There are a thousand and one details to be settled.

The rabbi must be consulted. An early talk with him is important for an understanding of Jewish marriage concepts, as well as for making arrangements for "the day." Do this before making other commitments.

"HOME IS AN ALTAR"

THE HEBREW TERM FOR MARRIAGE, *kiddushin,* meaning "holiness," is a key to the Jewish attitude toward the relationship between husband and wife. Marriage, in the Jewish view, is a sacred and beautiful joining together of two people who love each other. It is much more than a social institution with biological, psychological and economic bases.

From the Jewish point of view husband and wife are regarded as equals. The two people building a home together are expected to make adjustments to each other in their sexual relationship as well as in their social, personal and financial needs. All questions of marital relationship and family life—financial matters, legal status, and, especially, physical well-being—are worked out in detail in Jewish law.

For information on the subject of *niddah* (separation during the menstrual period) you may want to read the section on marital laws in *The Jewish Woman and Her Home* by Hyman E. Goldin, published by the Hebrew Publishing Company.

Jewish traditional literature stresses the give-and-take of the marriage bond. The laws governing the husband's relation to his wife are based on a tender and respectful attitude toward her as a woman, wife and mother. This is exemplified by the ancient custom of the husband chanting a hymn of praise to her on Friday evening before the Shabbat dinner—*eshet ḥayil,* "Woman of Worth" (Proverbs 31:10-31).

THE WEDDING DAY

AN OLD CUSTOM REQUIRES THE BRIDE AND GROOM to fast on the wedding day until the ceremony, except on those days like the Sabbath and Rosh Hodesh when fasting is forbidden. This custom, like the fast on Yom Kippur, suggests spiritual self-purification before embarking on a new life.

Whether the wedding is held at home or in the rabbi's study, whether it involves an elaborate procession in the synagogue or is a religious pageant in the ballroom, the ceremony should be performed under a *huppah* (canopy). More and more, the wedding ceremony takes place at the synagogue or in the home. The keynote should be dignity, good taste and reverence.

There is no order fixed by Jewish law for the procession. The arrangements are worked out by the family and the rabbi. It is interesting to note that, according to Jewish custom, the bride is not "given away," but is accompanied to the altar by her father or by both of her parents. The bride stands at the right hand of the groom, suggested by the verse "at thy right hand doth stand the queen" (Psalms 45:10).

Whether there are a dozen bridesmaids, ushers and flower girls, or merely a single attendant, is incidental. The ceremony itself is simple. The rabbi conducting the services may vary the details, but essentially the traditional marriage service consists of the following:

The welcoming benediction to the bride and groom.

The blessing over the first cup of wine.

The placing of the ring on the forefinger of the bride's right hand.

The reading of the marriage contract (*ketubah*).

The chanting of the seven blessings (*sheva berahot*).

The breaking of a glass by the groom.

THE HUPPAH   The *huppah* or marriage canopy may be taken to symbolize the union of bride and groom under one roof and the new home to be established. It is sometimes made of silk or velvet; it may even be a floral arrangement. The four poles may be held by four men, who are given this function as an honor.

THE RING   The wedding ring should be a band with no diamonds or other precious stones. Handsome rings with Hebrew inscriptions are available, if you are interested in a ring with a Jewish motif. Your Sisterhood gift shop will know where you can buy one. If you are thinking of holding a double-ring ceremony, a comparatively recent innovation, be sure to learn the opinion of the rabbi who will officiate.

COVER THE HEAD   At a traditional Jewish wedding the groom wears a head covering; the bride customarily wears a veil. Since all those present at the wedding are participants in a religious ceremony, rather than spectators at a performance, all the men should be provided with caps.

THE MELODY LINGERS ON   Music provides a pleasant background for the ceremony, if the selections are carefully made. There is nothing particularly sacred about the wedding marches from Wagner or Mendelssohn, or the song "Oh, Promise Me." Many fine compositions by modern Jewish composers are available for solos, and for the processional and recessional. Consult the rabbi and cantor of your synagogue or temple for suggestions. The National Jewish Music Council at 15 East 26th Street, New York City, will also be helpful.

RECEPTION   Nothing should mar the beauty and the joyous mood of the wedding day. Plan the reception far in advance. Anticipate all details so that last-minute decisions don't make a nervous wreck of you. If entertainment is planned, select a program suitable to the significance of the occasion.

ב ה

קול ששון   זקול שמחה

קול חתן   וקול כלה

Dr. and Mrs. Alexander Joseph Davidson

request the honor of your presence

at the marriage of their daughter

Joy

to

Matthew Rubin

Lieutenant (j.g.) United States Naval Reserve

on Sunday the ninth of December

at eleven o'clock

The Chapel

Jewish Theological Seminary of America

New York

Reception

immediately following the ceremony

Hotel Madison

Fifteen East Seventy-ninth Street

New York

Kindly respond

45 East 82nd Street

New York, N.Y.

A variation of a formal wedding invitation, with Hebrew

The meal should start with the *motzi*, and grace should be recited at the end of the meal, followed again by the *sheva berahot*.

"Blessed be our God, in Whose abode is joy, of Whose bounty we have partaken, and through Whose goodness we live." (From the grace after the wedding feast.)

DO speak to the rabbi about the wedding date and plans, making sure that he is available and that there are no religious restrictions on the date you have set.

Arrange for the bride and groom to meet with the rabbi for a premarital interview. Both should be able to tell him their full Hebrew names.

Consult the laws of your state on marriage.

Refer to helpful bride's books like those listed in the bibliography at the end of this chapter.

Check your guest list carefully with *both* families.

Arrange for an "aufruf" on the Sabbath preceding the marriage. On this occasion, the bride and bridegroom attend services together and the bridegroom is called to the reading of the Torah.

Make sure, if the wedding is in a synagogue, that the attendants are dressed decorously.

Start the wedding ceremony on time.

Maintain the dignity and traditional beauty of the service.

Provide attractive little blessing and hymn books as mementos.

DON'T allow caterers, "marriage performers" or others to lead you into the showy and theatrical kind of wedding arrangements that can become a *hillul hashem* (desecration of God's name).

Don't serve food and drinks before the ceremony. The hilarity that may result is not appropriate to the religious nature of the occasion. The reception should follow the ceremony, when gaiety is in order.

Don't have photographs taken during the ceremony. The lights and the activity of the photographer spoil the religious mood and distract the assemblage. Pictures can be taken before and after the ceremony. A tape recorder, provided it is not in evidence, can provide a permanent record of the wedding.

DIVORCE

EVEN THE HAPPIEST OF MARRIAGES encounter times of stress and disagreement. Should these become serious, do not jump to the conclusion that the marriage is a failure. The first thing to do is to talk things over with the rabbi. Many a marriage has attained great happiness and stability after passing through stormy seas. The fact must be faced, however, that there are circumstances in which dissolution of the marriage is indicated. Judaism sanctions divorce, since it recognizes that husband and wife may find it unbearable to live together. At the same time, it is important to note that strong family ties, and the whole ethical content of Jewish life, have in the past kept the Jewish divorce rate low.

If a divorce does take place, it is vital for Jewish couples to remember this: just as the marriage ceremony is religious in nature, so also must a divorce include a religious dissolution of the bond, in addition to the civil procedure. The Jewish document of divorce is known as a *get*. Obviously, rabbinical guidance is indispenable in this area.

One final admonition must be added. Both husband and wife should make sure that the *get* procedure is carried through to its conclusion as soon as possible after the civil decree is made final. Failure to do so may jeopardize the possibility of remarriage.

FAMILY MILESTONES

BIRTHDAYS, GRADUATIONS, ANNIVERSARIES are all occasions for family joy *(simhot)*. The family usually celebrates with parties, gifts and cards. The synagogue, too, often takes note of these dates. The celebrants may be mentioned at a late Friday evening service during the month. Sometimes, children are called up for a blessing by the rabbi.

Again, in Jewish tradition, these are times for giving as well as receiving. Appropriate institutions might be given token gifts. The custom of planting a tree in Israel (through the Jewish National Fund) or giving a contribution to Youth Aliyah, is a good way to mark a birthday. Wedding anniversaries might well be occasions for family gatherings instead of just a "date" for husband and wife. Many couples feel that the wedding anniversary pro-

vides an ideal opportunity to express to the children the warmth
and happiness of a good marriage.

YOU MIGHT WANT TO REFER TO THESE

❦ IF YOU ARE A NEW OR EXPECTANT MOTHER

OUR BABY by Sadie Rose Weilerstein (Women's League) is a
book you may want to own or give as a gift. It is an artistically illustrated "baby book" for keeping a record of the
baby's first five years. In addition to the usual material found
in such books, this one contains items of special Jewish
interest.

THE BLESSED EVENT by Rabbi Hyman Chanover (Jonathan David)
is a small helpful booklet which gives information on names, ceremonies associated with birth, etc. Remember also *These Are the
Names* mentioned on page 33.

YOU AND YOUR ADOPTED CHILD by Eda J. LeShan is an informative
booklet (Public Affairs Committee, 381 Park Avenue South, New
York   N. Y.)

NOTE: The Women's League has an "illuminated" certificate
to be sent as a card on the birth of a baby boy or girl (see page
38).

❦ FOR YOUR YOUNGSTER TO READ

WITH THE JEWISH CHILD IN HOME AND SYNAGOGUE by Elma E. Levinger (Bloch Publishing Company). Customs and ceremonies described in an informal style to arouse the interest of children in the
8 to 10 age group.

JEWISH CUSTOMS AND CEREMONIES by Ben M. Ediden (Hebrew Publishing Company). A popular discussion of the origin and significance of ceremonial practices in the home and synagogue for the
12 to 16 year old.

THE BAR MITZVAH TREASURY edited by Azriel Eisenberg (Behrman
House). This excellent anthology of literary treasures of past and
present includes selections on God, man, Torah, Israel, etc., and
would make a good Bar Mitzvah gift. The Katsh anthology mentioned on page 13 (Chapter 1) is another suitable book.

❦ FOR THE BRIDE-TO-BE

YOUR WEDDING by Marjorie Binford Woods (Bobbs Merrill Company)
gives general information and practical advice on invitations, announcements, receptions and other important details.

THE BRIDE'S REFERENCE BOOK by the editors of Bride's Magazine (M. Barrows & Co.) is a helpful, readable book for many aspects of home management, presented by experts in an attractive format and charming style.

THE COMPLETE BOOK OF ETIQUETTE by Amy Vanderbilt (Doubleday and Company), subtitled "A Guide to Gracious Living," has sections on weddings and other functions. The information given on Jewish practices should be rechecked with a rabbi.

✿ FOR THE BRIDE OR THE WIFE

The following books on marriage may be helpful references for the married as well as the about-to-be.

MARRIAGE MADE IN HEAVEN by Rabbi Nathan Drazin (Abelard-Schuman). This marriage-counselling handbook written by an orthodox rabbi is a candid guide to marital relations, written with sympathy and understanding. One reviewer said it includes "ancient rules and modern psychiatry."

MEANING OF MARRIAGE AND THE FOUNDATIONS OF THE FAMILY by Sidney E. Goldstein (Bloch Publishing Company).

THE JEWISH WOMAN AND HER HOME by Hyman Goldin (Hebrew Publishing Company). Comprehensive outline of laws and customs for the Orthodox woman.

A JEWISH CHILD IS BORN by Nathan Gottlieb (Bloch). Among the subjects discussed are: History and Ritual of Circumcision—Redemption of the Firstborn—Adoption—Conversion—Choosing and Giving of Names.

NOTE: The United Synagogue of America publishes an excellent series of pamphlets on Bar Mitzvah, Bat Mitzvah, Jewish education and marriage.

CHAPTER 4

A Time of Mourning

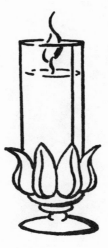

"The memory of the righteous shall be for a blessing"
(Proverbs 10:7)

— 4 —

A Time of Mourning

"THERE IS A TIME TO WEEP . . . a time to mourn" (Ecclesiastes 3.4) expresses the Jewish belief that death is part of life. The Jew looks at death realistically; he accepts it as inevitable. Judaism respects grief and provides for its emotional release.

All of us at some time meet the tragedy involved in losing a member of the family, a friend or neighbor. Even before the sense of loss is realized, there are bewildering questions of what to do, to whom to turn. As soon as the relatives have been informed of the death, the rabbi should be called. His counsel will ease the burden of arrangements for the funeral and burial service. He will also answer questions on the Jewish attitude toward immortality and death, on special problems such as postponement of burial, or on shrouds *(taḥriḥim)*.

BURIAL

THE FIRST CONCERN OF THE MOURNERS is the proper interment of the body. Today, most services are conducted in the funeral chapel. The body is prepared for burial according to Jewish law called *taharah* (purity) and is buried as soon after death as possible. Jewish tradition strongly disapproves of cremation. "And the dust returneth to the earth as it was, and the spirit returneth unto God who gave it" (Ecclesiastes 12.7). A light is kindled at the head of the bier to symbolize the immortality of the soul.

Everything connected with the funeral is kept simple. Sometimes chapels introduce practices not in accord with Jewish beliefs, and the mourners accept the suggestions because they do not know the tradition, or because they are afraid they may not do enough for the memory of the departed, or because in their grief they succumb to the pressures of salesmanship. Elaborate caskets, floral arrangements and melodramatic innovations are out of place. Your rabbi is your best adviser here.

MOURNING

JEWISH MOURNING OBSERVANCES have a sound psychological basis. Mourning is obligatory for the direct relatives of the deceased— father, mother, husband, wife, son, daughter, brother or sister. Immediately before the funeral, a part of the clothing of the mourner is cut or torn. This is called *kriah*. Some rabbis permit the cutting of a black ribbon, which has been pinned to the lapel, in observance of this rite. The *kriah* is performed with the mourners standing up, to impress upon them that they should stand up to life's sorrows and problems. The mourners say: "Blessed art Thou, o Lord our God, King of the Universe, Whose judgments are true."

Mourning is divided into three periods—shivah, the first seven days—the concentrated period of mourning; *sheloshim*, the first thirty days, during which entertainments also are forbidden; and the eleven months, during which the kaddish (memorial prayer) is recited.

Young children should be permitted but not forced to participate in some aspects of the rituals of grief. They should be allowed to attend the funeral if they wish. Of course, parental discretion is called for. The children should be encouraged to help in small ways during the shivah period.

CUSTOMS OBSERVED DURING SHIVAH   After the funeral, mourners are expected to remain at home, except for attending Friday evening and Sabbath services at the synagogue.

Whenever possible, morning and evening services should be

held daily in the home during the shivah; otherwise the mourners join the minyan in the synagogue.

A light in memory of the departed is kept burning throughout the week. Special candles or lamps may be obtained from the synagogue or funeral chapel.

The first meal following the return from the cemetery customarily includes hard-boiled eggs and bread, symbols of life and hope. Wine or meat is never served at this time. This first meal is prepared by friends.

Mourners may prepare or cook meals for their own use, but serving visitors is out of place.

It is customary for the bereaved to sit on low chairs or stools. This practice is one of the ancient Hebrew symbols of mourning.

Wearing black is not mandatory.

The custom of covering mirrors is not explicit in Jewish law.

Customs associated with mourning do not apply on the Sabbath or on festivals. All overt symbols of mourning should be removed on these days.

Marital relations are forbidden during the shivah week.

There are special rules governing the termination of shivah by the occurrence of a festival, and the observance of mourning by one who gets belated news of bereavement. In these and similar cases, a rabbi should be consulted.

VISITING THE HOUSE OF MOURNING Visitors are sometimes embarrassed because they don't know what to say or how to act. The traditional words of consolation are simple—

הַמָּקוֹם יְנַחֵם אֶתְכֶם בְּתוֹךְ שְׁאָר אֲבֵלֵי צִיּוֹן וִירוּשָׁלָיִם:

("May the Almighty comfort you and all the mourners of Zion and Jerusalem.") The visitor who does not know Hebrew might say, "May God comfort you." Of course, any spontaneous expression of sympathy is in place. Sometimes, silence is eloquent; use your judgment. But one should not refrain from talking about the deceased; on the contrary, such talk is a source of comfort.

There is often a question of what to bring. This is not a time for gift-giving in the ordinary sense. Elaborate fruit baskets, boxes of candy and personal gifts are inappropriate. Helping with the household cooking is another matter; it is a kind act to prepare something for a meal. Bringing a book for reflective reading is considerate. In place of flowers or similar gifts, contributing to the favorite charity of the deceased, presenting a prayer book to the synagogue, planting a tree in Israel, or giving to other worthy causes in memory of the dead, would certainly be appreciated by the mourners.

IN MEMORIAM

THE FAMILY AT THIS TIME may want to express its grief by some worthy act—perhaps a contribution to the synagogue or to a theological seminary, an educational foundation, Hadassah, the United Jewish Appeal, the Jewish National Fund, the local Jewish philanthropy, or a medical research fund. They might place a memorial tablet in the synagogue, or include the name of the departed in the congregation's book of remembrance.

Visiting the cemetery is purely a personal matter. It is recommended, however, that one should not go until after the period of *sheloshim*. The unveiling of the tombstone takes place preferably after the eleven months of mourning. No elaborate ceremony is required; friends and relatives may be asked to come.

THE KADDISH The kaddish (sanctification) is recited by the sons every day for eleven months. The daughters, or anyone else wishing to pay loving tribute, may also recite this prayer. Though the kaddish is recited in memory of the departed, it is significant that it contains no reference to death. In this prayer, we publicly praise God, renewing our faith in the worthwhileness of life, despite the anguish of bereavement. We proclaim our desire to continue the tradition that binds generation to generation, and express the hope that the day will come when the world will be at peace.

It is customary, in speaking of the deceased, to add *"alav hashalom"* ("peace be upon him"), or *"aleha hashalom"* ("peace be upon her").

"YAHRZEIT" "Yahrzeit" is the anniversary of the death according to the Jewish calendar; a *lu'ah* is helpful in determining the civil date. It is a widespread custom to keep a memorial lamp burning from sunset to sunset on this anniversary. Those observing the "yahrzeit" are expected to recite kaddish at the services on this day. Often, the occasion is marked by the giving of charity.

CONDOLENCE CARDS A word on condolence cards and their acknowledgment might be helpful here. A personal note sincerely expressing regret and offering friendship at the time of loss is most satisfactory. When a printed card is purchased, it should be as simple and dignified as possible, without long maudlin messages. Some Jewish organizations offer appropriate cards, usually sent by them to acknowledge a contribution made in memory of the dead.

In answer to messages of condolence, again the personal note is best. When a printed form is used, it should be dignified. The form on this page, sent by a bereaved family, may suggest other possibilities.

There are many beautiful and comforting expressions on the subject of death in the Bible, the Talmud and prayer book. This one from the Talmud is worth remembering—"There are those who gain eternity in a lifetime; others, in one brief hour."

פיה פתחה בחכמה
ותורת חסד על לשונה

She opened her mouth with wisdom and the law of loving kindness was on her tongue.

PROVERBS 31:26

The children of Bessie Greenberg deeply appreciate your expression of sympathy and friendship at the passing of their beloved Mother

May the Lord bless you and your dear ones and keep you from sorrow

A dignified acknowledgment of expressions of condolence

THESE PAMPHLETS MAY BE HELPFUL

IN TIMES OF SORROW by Dr. Albert Gordon (United Synagogue of America). A clearly presented series of questions and answers on the burial service and the rites of mourning. Also includes prayers and words of comfort.

THOUGHTS ON BEREAVEMENT AND GRIEF by Dr. Jeshaia Schnitzer (United Synagogue Commission on Marriage and the Family). A sound exposition on the Jewish traditional attitude toward death and an explanation of the significance of mourning practices.

WHEN YOU LOSE A LOVED ONE—a Public Affairs Pamphlet (22 East 38th Street, New York, N. Y. Although this pamphlet is written from the general and not the Jewish point of view, it includes particularly helpful discussions on telling children about death, children attending a funeral, etc., as well as adult reactions to the death of a loved one.

❦ THIS BOOK MIGHT BE GIVEN TO A MOURNER

A TREASURY OF COMFORT by Sidney Greenberg (Crown Publishers). A rabbi's anthology of prose and poetry, selected to give solace and comfort to the bereaved.

A MODERN TREASURY OF JEWISH THOUGHTS edited by Sidney Greenberg (Yoseloff).

HEART OF WISDOM by Bernard Raskas (Burning Bush Press). A thought for each day of the Jewish year.

CHAPTER 5

The Sabbath

"I have a precious gift in my treasure house and Sabbath is its name" (Talmud)

5

The Sabbath

How to "Remember the Sabbath to Keep it Holy."

B Y NOW YOU REALIZE THAT YOU SHARE many responsibilities
and *mitzvot* with your husband. Indeed, you are the one
who has the rare privilege of ushering peace into your
home. You actually can change the pace of the week, hush the
noises of the shops, the street, the world, for a brief span of time.

Standing quietly in front of your Sabbath candles, surrounded
by your family, you can set the mood for tranquillity. The wheels
stop whirring, the tumult is silenced, and a time for rest and
change, for revitalization and refreshment is upon your household.
The Sabbath is a home-centered holiday; it is only natural that
the Jewish woman should be responsible for preserving this day.

SHALOM BAYIT   When the Sabbath is properly observed, parents are more relaxed. Tradition recognizes that on the Sabbath
husband and wife are at their greatest receptivity for marital
intimacy and tender devotion. The general home atmosphere is
uplifted and the true sense of *shalom bayit* (peace at home) and
kedushah (holiness) pervades its walls. It is the time of week when
parents and children should show particular concern for one another. The friendly atmosphere is contagious.

How to "Observe the Sabbath to Keep it Holy"

THE HOUSE IS SPOTLESS, the humdrum weekly routine is halted, the delicious aromatic "Shabbos" meal prepared, the family dressed for dinner. The table is set with your best linen and china, silver and glassware; the candlesticks are polished, the kiddush cup and wine decanter in place. The two hallahs are covered with a cloth or napkin. The wife lights the candles, shades her eyes from their light with her hands—the magic of the Sabbath is about to begin.

COUNT YOUR BLESSINGS

SHE RECITES THE BLESSING (page 239) and perhaps adds, silently, a short personal prayer, thanking God for the joy of the week and for the Sabbath. In many homes, the father blesses the children, placing his hands on their heads. For the sons, he says, *"yesimeha elohim ke'efrayim vehimenasheh."* ("May the Lord bless you as He blessed Ephraim and Menassah.") For the daughters: *"yesimeh elohim kesarah rivkah rahel vele'ah."* ("May the Lord bless you as He blessed Sarah, Rebecca, Rachel and Leah.") Just before dinner *"shalom aleihem malahei hasharet"* ("Peace be unto you") is sung by the entire family from the prayer book.

AT THE TABLE

THE FAMILY GATHERS AT THE TABLE, the wine is poured into the goblet, and kiddush (sanctification of the day—page 241) is recited, usually by the father. After the washing of the hands, *hamotzi* (thanksgiving for bread—page 243) is spoken and a small piece of hallah is given to each person at the table. One does not speak after *hamotzi* until the bread has been tasted.

In this prelude to the Sabbath, there are many variant customs. In some families, all present participate in the kiddush, in whole or in part. Sometimes, children who have learned the kiddush are allowed to say it in turn. It is a good practice.

The wine, like the bread, is shared around the table. The father may pour a little from the kiddush goblet into the glass of everyone present. Very young children may be given some grape juice or a drop of wine in their water.

The Sabbath meal is then served. It should be especially relaxed and unhurried. A fine old custom, far too often neglected, is the singing of *zemirot* (table hymns) between courses. *Birkat hamazon* (grace) is recited. See the table of contents of almost any prayer book. Both words and music can be found in *Sabbath, the Day of Delight* by Abraham E. Millgram (see end of this chapter).

IN THE SYNAGOGUE

TRADITIONAL FRIDAY EVENING SERVICES are held at sundown before the meal. In communities where there are late Friday evening services, the family goes as a group. Sometimes the service is followed by an Oneg Shabbat (joy of the Sabbath), a social hour.

On Shabbat morning, dressed in their "holiday best," the family should go to the synagogue services. Everyone should dress appropriately, women should remember to wear hats. No packages or gifts should be carried to the synagogue. You, as the housewife, may have to leave for the synagogue a little later than the others, but be sure to be on time for the Torah reading.

SHABBAT AFTERNOON

HOME FROM THE SERVICE, it is time to enjoy the Sabbath dinner. There is a shorter kiddush to say; again *hamotzi* is followed by the meal. Once more, *zemirot* are in order, and then the grace after meals. Then the members of the family can settle down to rest, nap, read or study, or to other quiet activities. Sabbath afternoon is a good time for a pleasant visit to nearby friends. In some synagogues, there is a study hour before or after the brief Sabbath afternoon service.

HAVDALLAH (Farewell to the Sabbath)

"Dear Sabbath Day doth now depart—
May the coming week be blessed
With good fortune and good deeds."
—Old Yiddish hymn for the housewife

Twilight approaches and the Sabbath is about to depart. As soon as night falls, is it time for *havdallah* (literally, separation), a brief ceremony dramatic for children and significant for adults. Just as the arrival of the sacred day was celebrated in the kiddush, so is its departure now proclaimed in this prayer which gives thanks for the rhythms of time and of life.

For *havdallah* you will need a cup of wine, a little aromatic spice, and a lighted candle. Customarily, it is the man of the house who recites the *havdallah*. At the blessing for the spices, he passes the spice-box around so that all present may inhale the fragrance. Similarly, at the blessing for the light, those present place their hands in its glow. At the conclusion of the ceremony, the wine is shared.

It is traditional for the youngest child to hold the *havdallah* candle; another child holds the spice-box. In large families, parents may wish to rotate the honors from week to week.

There are many other customs which add symbolic beauty to the *havdallah* service. The wine cup, for example, should be filled to the brim, or even overflow slightly, as the augury of a week brimful of blessings. For this reason, goblets especially designed for *havdallah* usually come with a small saucer. And the candle should have more than one wick, corresponding to the plural "lights" in the benediction. Special *havdallah* candles, woven in many colorful strands, are available in most Jewish bookstores. The candle should be extinguished after the ceremony, and ought to last for many weeks.

Indeed, this ceremony has given birth to a wide variety of lovely ceremonial objects. The well-equipped Jewish home should have a *havdallah* spice-box, candle, and, if possible, a special goblet. For spices, a mixture of cloves, nutmeg, and bay leaf is suggested.

The twilight moments before *havdallah* are appropriate for a family sing, with *zemirot* and other songs of gentle mood. And after *havdallah*, the greeting is *"shavu'a tov"* ("good week") or the popular Yiddish equivalent "gut voch." Words and music for the service itself can be found in Millgram's *The Sabbath,* and there are other appropriate songs in the same book.

The Sabbath is the oldest of all the Jewish Holy Days and the one most honored. It is the only one mentioned in the Ten Commandments. The name "Saturday" does not convey the spirit of the Sabbath.

Even if we reach a four-day work week, we shall still need the special quality of the Sabbath. It is not merely a day of physical rest; it uplifts the spirit. It is not a day of abstentions and gloom. The Sabbath alerts all the senses to beauty and wholesomeness. It is an Oneg—a delight, an enrichment.

Tradition has always described the Sabbath as a Queen—Shabbat Hamalkah. At the very beginning of the Friday evening service, the Sabbath is also welcomed as a bride. It is with good reason that the woman is devoted to the Sabbath.

SABBATH SIDELIGHTS

The proper greeting for the Sabbath is *"shabbat shalom"* ("a peaceful Sabbath"), or "Gut Shabbos" ("a good Sabbath").

In many homes it is customary, just before the kindling of the Sabbath lights, to put coins in the Jewish National Fund or Torah Fund boxes, or in containers for various philanthropic endeavors. Let the children drop in the coins.

Some homes have reintroduced the recitation on Friday eve of that remarkable paean of praise from Proverbs (31:10-31)—*eshet hayil* (Woman of Worth). The English version might be read in part by a member of the family.

One explanation given for the two loaves of hallah is that they are symbolic of the double portion of the manna which was gathered by the Israelites in the desert on the eve of Sabbath (Exodus 16:4-5).

Sometimes a third meal of the Sabbath day, called "Shalosh Se'udos," is eaten in the vestry rooms of the synagogue. And in some homes, the family eats a fourth meal, the *melaveh malkah*, as a farewell to the Sabbath Queen.

"Young marrieds" go to their parents on Friday evenings or on holidays. It might be wise to reverse the procedure occasionally, with the parents as guests in their children's homes.

Raisins and nuts on the table are reminiscent of "old country" "Shabbos" refreshments.

Chess, Lotto and Scrabble are interesting games for all the family. Scores can be kept without writing by placing cards inside books at page numbers corresponding to the scores.

Songs to sing and books to read make pleasant diversions. See page 69 for other suggestions.

ONEG SHABBAT   Another custom associated with the Sabbath is the Oneg Shabbat (joy of the Sabbath), an informal celebration, held after late Friday evening services or at home on Saturday afternoon. Refreshments are served, songs are sung, and appropriate programs arranged. Isaiah urged the people to "call the Sabbath a delight" (Isaiah 58:13). The Oneg Shabbat has its roots in the "Shalosh Se'udos" custom.

The modern Oneg Shabbat originated in Palestine. The poet Hayim Nahman Bialik started the custom in Tel Aviv, where he led informal discussions on Sabbath afternoons, followed by group singing and concluding with the *havdallah*. This pleasant custom was then introduced in America. Sisterhoods and other groups often sponsor such afternoon gatherings. If a child's birthday occurs on the Sabbath, this occasion can be an Oneg Shabbat.

❧ GIFTS OF THE SEASON

Attractive wine markers in silver, bearing the inscription *bore peri hagafen*, are available in Jewish bookstores and gift shops.

Collapsible silver or brass candlesticks, to use when traveling, make an excellent gift for the woman who "has everything." They can be ordered through your Sisterhood book or gift shop and are available in some of the independent Jewish shops.

The Sabbath, by A. J. Heschel (Farrar, Straus and Cudahy), gives a poetic description of that day.

Other suitable gifts are coasters for kiddush cups, a tray for the wine decanter, a hallah knife or tray, a *havdallah* tray.

CANDLE LIGHTING

Take note of these points about the candles:

1. Suitable candles for the Sabbath come in two sizes—one size long enough for summer evenings and the other slightly longer for winter use. They are less expensive than fancy tapers and are packed in boxes by the dozen or in small cartons of seventy-two or one hundred and forty-four candles. These are generally labeled Sabbath candles and can be purchased in grocery stores and five-and-tens or may be ordered through your Sisterhood gift shops. The candles should be white.

2. If you place a little water in each holder, the candle will burn down to the very end as required, and still not damage your candlesticks. There are also small holders—glass or metal *bobêches*—that may be placed in the average size candlesticks for similar protection. Aluminum foil wrapped around the bottom of the candles can also be used.

3. As a rule, two candles are lit, although some women follow a family custom of lighting one candle for each member of the family.

4. Small girls often have their own miniature candlesticks, to be "like Mother" in reciting the *berahah* (blessing).

5. If you have a guest, you may invite her to light additional candles with you, though it is not mandatory that she do so.

DO take note of these points about *hallot*:

The *hallot* may be any shape—sometimes they are oblong, braided or twisted.

If you bake your own *hallot*, set aside a small piece of dough, reciting the blessing on page 241.

If you buy *hallot*, remember to buy two unsliced loaves for each Sabbath meal. If large *hallot* are impractical for the small family, you might buy two small rolls twisted like *hallot* for each meal. A sliced hallah is permissible for general table use.

Conserve your energy for the Sabbath by making all preparations and doing all shopping, cooking and baking long before sunset on Friday.

Give the boys and girls in the family definite responsibilities like polishing the candlesticks, preparing the wine decanter and kiddush cups, or setting the table.

Consult your *lu'ah* (calendar) for candle lighting time. Approximately twenty minutes before sunset is the stipulated time.

Invite some friend who is without family, or some newcomers in the neighborhood, as guests for the Sabbath.

Recite the blessings in Hebrew. There is a distinct value both in the practice of speaking Hebrew and as a reminder that this is a sacred tongue.

Provide enough *kipot* (caps) for the menfolk.

Try to avoid quarrels and unpleasant or painful situations.

Encourage your children to participate in the Junior Congregation.

Take a walk and visit with family and friends.

Set aside time for reading aloud, or alone, or for quiet games.

Guard against fatigue.

Be a model of calm and quiet.

DON'T let a maid substitute for you and light your candles. Be home on time and *do it yourself.*

Don't blow out the candles; let them burn out themselves.

Don't use table mats or informal cloths. The occasion calls for a handsome cloth, preferably white.

Don't serve Friday night kiddush in another room away from the table.

Don't allow your family or "help" to do heavy chores or housework on the Sabbath.

Don't cook or bake. Heating arrangements should be made in advance.

Don't make appointments for beauty salons, music lessons, or other everyday activities.

Don't accept social or business engagements for the Sabbath. "We always have dinner with the family on 'Shabbos'" is a good answer to such invitations.

✣ BASIC SHABBAT MENUS

There is by no means only one type of traditional meal for Shabbat, but certain foods have been associated with the day. It is interesting to note that in England, fried fish is the special Friday night dish; in the Orient, a dairy meal is customary. There are infinite variations. We include here one that is traditional with families of eastern European background. An asterisk indicates recipe in Chapter 17.

SABBATH EVE MEAL

Fruit Salad
Soup with Noodles or Rice
Roast or Boiled Chicken
Potato Kugel (pudding)°
Carrots and Peas
Strudel ° or Compote or Sherbet
Tea or Black Coffee

In some families, gefillte fish is traditional, even at meat meals.

IF YOU PREFER FISH—A DAIRY MEAL

Fruit
Cream Soup
Gefillte Fish,° Fried Fish or Sweet and Sour Fish
Noodle Pudding °
Vegetable Salad
Fruit Mold   Cookies
Coffee

A SHABBAT NOON MEAL

Juice or Fruit
Borscht (cold or hot)
Cold Brisket of Beef
Salad   Asparagus
Cake
Tea or Black Coffee

❧ A CHILD'S SABBATH BIRTHDAY PARTY

Keep the Shabbat atmosphere by having appropriate games and re-freshments. The birthday candles should not be lighted until after *havdallah.*

TABLE SETTING SUGGESTIONS

White cloth with blue paper napkins.

Shabbat decorated cloth and napkins (from Sisterhood book or gift shops).

Plastic cloth which can be decorated earlier in the week by the child, using Shabbat symbols.

CENTERPIECE

Fruit or flowers on the birthday cake or paper crown suggesting the Queen Sabbath

SUGGESTED MENU

Grapejuice Punch

Egg Kichel (any Jewish bakery)
filled with egg or other salad

or

Hallah slices with gefillte fish

or

Small open face sandwiches cut as stars

Cookies made with holiday cookie cutters

or

Cupcakes iced with blue and white frosting

FOR THE SIGNIFICANCE OF THE SABBATH

SABBATH, THE DAY OF DELIGHT by Abraham E. Millgram (Jewish Publication Society) is worth owning. In addition to a perceptive discussion of the meaning of the Sabbath, this fine book includes essays, stories, poetry, music and program material on the Sabbath.

THE SABBATH BOOK by Samuel M. Segal (Thomas Yoseloff) gives the story of the Sabbath, legends, customs and ceremonies.

NOTE: Most of the Festival books listed in Chapter 8 include a chapter on the Sabbath.

FOR READING TO CHILDREN—See the listing of children's books in the general bibliography on page 240.

CHAPTER 6

The Yearly Round

*"So teach us to number our days, that we may get us a heart
of wisdom" (Psalms 90:12)*

6

The Yearly Round

HAVE YOU EVER WONDERED WHY Jewish Festivals seem to wander about the calendar? Why Rosh Hashanah, for example, comes in September one year, but in October the next year? Or why anniversaries, like a "yahrzeit" or a Bar Mitzvah, vary from the original date in the civil calendar? It is not because they are not fixed dates, but rather because they are fixed by a different calendar—the Jewish calendar.

Mankind has had many calendars, a number of which are still in use—the Gregorian, the Moslem, the Chinese, the Jewish, to mention a few. After all, a calendar is merely a system of keeping time in large units, such as months or years. And man's timekeepers for this purpose have been the wonderfully regular heavenly bodies, principally the sun and the moon.

From the moon, with its dramatic waxing and waning, we get the idea of the month; from the sun, which governs the cycle of seasons, we get the time-unit known as the year. So it comes about that calendars are of two kinds—solar (sun) calendars, and lunar (moon) calendars. The civil, or Gregorian calendar, so widely used today throughout the world, is a solar calendar. The Moslem calendar is a purely lunar one, disregarding the seasons. The Jewish calendar is a combination of both, basically lunar, but adjusted to the solar year.

THE SUN AND THE MOON

THE MOON MAKES ITS JOURNEY around the earth, from one new moon to the next, in just about twenty-nine and a half days. Since we can't manage with fractional days, some months in the Jewish calendar have twenty-nine days, while some have thirty. So far, so good. But twelve times around gives us a year of only three hundred fifty-four days—a little more than eleven days short of the solar year, the time it takes the earth to get around the sun. To keep from getting out of kilter with the seasons, without abandoning the lunar month, there is only one thing to do. Let

After floor mosaic of the Zodiac at Beth-Alpha Synagogue, Palestine. Sixth century C.E.

the "deficit" accumulate for a bit, then have a leap year, by adding a whole month—a thirteenth month.

Of course, this makes it sound quite simple—which it isn't. There are lots of details to take care of—such as making sure that Yom Kippur doesn't fall on a Friday or a Sunday (that *would* be awkward!). As a matter of fact, three of the months vary in length, 29 days in some years, 30 in others. Plain years also vary—353, 354, or 355 days. And the leap years occur on the 3rd, 6th, 8th, 11th, 14th, 17th and 19th years of a cycle! They vary in length, too—383, 384, or 385 days.

Fortunately for you, you don't have to figure all this out for yourself. All you need do is get yourself a *lu'aḥ* (Jewish calendar) for the current year, and you will have before you all of the dates, together with corresponding days of the civil calendar. As with ordinary calendars, the *lu'aḥ* comes in a variety of forms—wall, pocket, desk, illustrated, plain or fancy. They are published by religious and charitable organizations, Jewish book dealers, business houses and many others. If you have any difficulty in getting one, ask at your synagogue.

A BIT OF HISTORY

KEEPING TIME BY THE MOON was the usual thing in the ancient Middle East; the Israelites were no exception. Indeed, the Christian holiday, Easter, is still calculated in relation to the moon, which explains why it coincides more often than not with Passover.

There were no published calendars in ancient Israel. It was the duty of the High Court in Jerusalem (Sanhedrin) to declare that the new moon had been sighted, and that another month had begun. High on the hilltops around Jerusalem, bonfires had been made ready; as soon as the signal was received, the fires were lit. From hilltop to hilltop the message passed, and by morning the whole country knew that Rosh Hodesh (the beginning of a new month) had arrived.

To inform the Jewish communities in other lands, messengers were dispatched; but the journey was long, and a festival might arrive before the messengers did. Therefore, the Jews outside of Palestine, uncertain of the exact date, observed each Festival for *two* days.

No doubt the Sanhedrin, with the passing centuries, had accumulated enough data to fix the calendar accurately in advance; but the practice of formal declaration was continued because it helped to maintain the unity of a scattered people. Finally, in the fourth century of the present era, when most of Jewry had been living outside of Palestine for hundreds of years, Hillel II, one of the last heads of the Sanhedrin, published the calendar in its present form.

But the age-old custom of announcing the new month persisted; and to this day, the coming of the new moon is declared in the synagogue on the preceding Sabbath, accompanied by the prayer that it be a time of blessing and peace. Another old custom has also persisted; to this day, Jews outside of Israel observe an extra day of each Festival (Pesach, Shavuot, and Sukkot). The practice has, however, been discontinued by Reform Jews.

NIGHT AND DAY

WHEN DOES A NEW DAY BEGIN? The civil calendar says "at midnight." The Jewish calendar says "at sunset." This is based on the phrase in the first chapter of the Torah: "God called the light day, and the darkness He called night; there was evening, there was morning—the first day" (Genesis 1.5). First evening, then morning —all part of the same day. This explains why the Sabbath begins on Friday at sundown, and why all holy days—indeed, all dates in the Jewish calendar—begin the evening before. This will affect important dates in your personal life—like the day for your baby's *brit*, the Hebrew date on your marriage certificate, or the dating of a "yahrzeit" for a loved one.

The whole subject of the calendar is a fascinating one. If you and your children are interested, you might consult *The Jewish Encyclopedia* for more information. You might also read *The Story of the Jewish Calendar* by Azriel Eisenberg (published by Abelard Schuman) which gives a full explanation of the Jewish calendar, discusses the difference between the solar and lunar calendars, and relates stories of the people who played a part in the development of the Jewish calendar.

CHAPTER 7

Holy Days and Holidays: I

ROSH HASHANAH
AND YOM KIPPUR

"These are the seasons of the Lord. . . ." (Leviticus 23:10)

THE SABBATH IS THE MODEL for the five other main sacred occasions of the Jewish year. As a matter of fact, they too, are called "Sabbaths," and share some of the characteristics of the weekly day of rest. They too, are ushered in with the lighting of candles at sundown, followed by kiddush and a festive Sabbathlike meal. Of course, each of them has its own special theme and significance; each of them its particular observances and traditions in home and synagogue. But all of them, in varying degree, call for abstention from workaday labors and all of them are ended with *havdallah.*

The five may be conveniently divided into two groups—the Days of Awe popularly called High Holy Days, and the Three Festivals. The Days of Awe are Rosh Hashanah and Yom Kippur. The Three Festivals are Sukkot, Pesach, and Shavuot.

There are, to be sure, other feasts and fasts in the Jewish calendar which are *not* "Sabbaths"—days like Purim, Hanukkah, Tishah B'Av. They will be dealt with separately.

7

Rosh Hashanah and Yom Kippur

"May all Thy children unite in one fellowship
To do Thy will with all their heart. . . ."
(Service for the Days of Awe)

THE SUMMER IS OVER, the pace of life quickens, and a new year is about to begin in the Jewish calendar. It begins in a mood of solemnity and high seriousness—no gloom, but certainly no frivolity. In the month of Tishri, the first month of the new year, the first ten days are set aside as the Ten Days of Penitence. They begin with Rosh Hashanah (New Year) on the first and second of Tishri, and end with Yom Kippur (Day of Atonement) on the tenth of the month.

This is a time for gentleness, for reflection and for personal stock-taking. Have the children had a long-standing quarrel? This is the time for them to "make up." Has a neighbor been offended? This is the time for a gesture of friendliness. Is there a relative who has been neglected? This is the time for a telephone call.

This is a time, too, for religious rededication. The moral and ethical teachings of Judaism, and its aspirations for universal brotherhood—themes present in every Jewish observance—are especially stressed in the prayers, the ceremonies, and the mood of these Holy Days.

Because of the season of the year in which it occurs, this may also be a time for opening new pages in the life of your family. The children will enter new classes when they return to school—both secular and religious. There may be a dramatic change from elementary school to high school; someone in the family may be starting college. You, too, will probably find your calendar beginning to fill up with meetings and social engagements.

GETTING READY

PREPARATION FOR THE SACRED SEASON traditionally starts thirty days in advance, at the beginning of the month of Elul, the last month of the old year. The shofar (ram's horn) sounds in the synagogue throughout that month. On the Saturday night immediately preceding Rosh Hashanah, a special penitential service, called *selihot,* is held at the synagogue, at midnight or sometime before dawn. Even the busy housewife tries to find time to attend this hour of reflection.

ROSH HASHANAH EVE

IT IS THE WOMAN OF THE HOUSE who ushers in the Holy Days by kindling the festive candles on both evenings of Rosh Hashanah, reciting the two blessings special to the occasion (page 239). The father and other members of the family should proceed to the synagogue for the evening service at sundown; the housewife may be too busy to attend this service. If she stays home, she should greet the returning worshippers with a cheerful *"leshanah tovah"* ("May it be a good year").

The table is set as for the Sabbath, with one additional feature —a plate of sliced apples and a dish of honey, symbolic of the hope that "the year may be a sweet one." The father chants the special kiddush for Rosh Hashanah found in the regular prayer book, and recites the *motzi* over the hallah. It is customary to dip a piece of sliced apple into the honey, saying, "May it be Thy will, oh Lord our God, to renew unto us a happy and pleasant new year." The meal then proceeds as on the Sabbath.

AT THE SYNAGOGUE

YOU WILL WANT TO JOIN YOUR FAMILY at the beautiful and impressive services on Rosh Hashanah morning. Make every effort to arrive early enough for the reading of the Torah, but, in any case, in time to hear the sound of the shofar which directly follows.

Because there are so many additional prayers for the Holy Days, it is necessary to use a special prayer book commonly called a Mahzor. Be sure there are enough copies for the members of the family.

It will help you to participate in the service if you familiarize yourself beforehand with some of the special aspects of the Mahzor. Certain editions offer not only a translation, but also instructive notes and explanations of the service. As on all Sabbaths and festive days, the morning service is threefold: *shaharit* (morning prayer); Scripture reading (Torah and prophets); and *musaf* (additional prayer).

It is in the *musaf* that you will find some, though by no means all, of the most dramatic sections of the service for the Days of Awe. In the *musaf* for Rosh Hashanah, for example, the central portion is devoted to three ideas fundamental to the Jewish religion. The first of these, called *malhuyot* (sovereignty), proclaims the kingship of God over the universe and over the affairs of man. The second, *zihronot* (remembrance), speaks of God in history and proclaims that there is no oblivion in His eternal memory for any aspect of the past. The third is *shofarot* (trumpets). It expresses faith in time to come, relating the Biblical references to the shofar, to aspirations for universal justice and peace, to the eternity of God's law, to hopes for the future of Israel, and to the trumpet of jubilee. After each of the three sections of the *musaf* have been read, the shofar is sounded.

The Mahzor will help you understand why Rosh Hashanah is also called "Day of Judgment," on which all God's children are judged; what is meant by the symbolic greeting "May you be inscribed in the Book of Life"; and many more of the ideas connected with this Holy Day which begins the Jewish year.

"AT HOME"

IN THE AFTERNOON, after the festive midday meal, it is customary to be "at home" to relatives and friends, to exchange Rosh Hashanah greetings and good wishes.

In the evening, the second day of Rosh Hashanah is ushered in exactly as the first. It is observed in the same manner, except that instead of the apples and honey, a new fruit is added, and the *sheheheyanu* (page 243) is recited.

SHABBAT SHUVAH   The Sabbath between Rosh Hashanah and Yom Kippur is called Shabbat Shuvah, because of the prophetic reading for the day (Hosea 14) which begins with the words *"shuvah yisrael,"* "Return, O Israel." It is also called Shabbat Teshuvah—the Sabbath of Repentance.

YOM KIPPUR

ON THE TENTH DAY OF TISHRI, Yom Kippur, the climax of the whole season is reached. This is the holiest day of the year, the Sabbath of Sabbaths. It is a day completely devoted to spiritual needs. The service in the synagogue starts just before sunset on the preceding day, and after a break for the night, is resumed in the morning and continues all day until nightfall. During this entire period, no food or drink is to be taken. Fasting helps us concentrate on our prayers and our self-examination. The Mahzor urges us to reflect on God's majesty and on human weakness, and to reflect frankly on our personal shortcomings. What is stressed is our capacity to improve our conduct and to live a better life.

The fast is a strain and often an ordeal. The woman's role is very important here. A feeling of calm, an understanding of special health needs, and careful planning far in advance will provide the sober, unhurried atmosphere which should precede the solemn day.

BEFORE THE FAST The day before Yom Kippur (Erev Yom Kippur) shares some of the sacred quality of the holy day. The afternoon service, while it is of the week-day variety, includes the confession of sins. The midday meal, which should be served early, is festive in its menu. Late in the afternoon, the family sits down at the table which has been set as for yom tov, although the candles are unlit and there is no kiddush. This is the meal before the fast. As on Rosh Hashanah, honey customarily appears on the table. Highly seasoned foods should not be served, in order to avoid intensifying thirst during the fast.

Shortly before sundown, the candles are lit and the blessing recited (page 242). If you follow the custom of lighting a "yahrzeit" (memorial) lamp in memory of a departed one, you should do it before kindling the Yom Kippur candles.

It is a lovely practice for parents to bless their children, before leaving for the synagogue. It can be done in silence while you place your hands on the child's bowed head.

KOL NIDRE EVE As you enter the synagogue, you may notice that the rabbi, cantor and some others may be wearing the long white robe that stands for purity and innocence. It is customary for the scrolls of the Torah to be draped in white mantles, the Ark to be covered with a white *parohet* (curtain), and the reading tables on the *bimah* decked with white covers. It is a holy evening.

The Ark is opened and the scrolls are taken out. The congregation rises and the *hazzan* sings the inspiring Kol Nidre (all vows) whose great antiquity and haunting melody have had a special appeal for the Jew throughout the ages. The hushed quality of Kol Nidre sets the mood for the rest of the service.

During the *ma'ariv* (evening) service, the special prayer *al het* (confessions) is introduced. It is interesting to note that all the confessions are in the plural to indicate that we are all responsible for one another.

YOM KIPPUR DAY Services continue in the synagogue throughout the next day. During the day, memorial prayers (yizkor) are said for the deceased relatives of individual families and for members of the congregation. Special prayers are sometimes included for the Jewish martyrs who lost their lives because of persecution or in defense of the community, for heroes of the Warsaw Ghetto and of the War of Independence in Israel, and for those who gave their lives fighting for our country.

The closing *(ne'ilah)* concludes the Yom Kippur service, but not before one long note is blown on the shofar and the congregation calls out *"leshanah haba'ah biyerushalayim."* "Next year in Jerusalem."

Now the *ma'ariv* service is chanted, at the end of which the *havdallah* ceremony is performed as on the Sabbath. Before leaving the synagogue, greetings are exchanged in the traditional words *"gemar ḥatimah tovah,"* "May you have a favorable verdict."

AT HOME At home a light meal is eaten, a "break the fast" meal (see page 93). Afterwards, friends and family often visit. In many homes, at this time, the first nail is driven in the sukkah in preparation for the joyous holiday of Sukkot, which is next in the Jewish calendar.

ROSH HASHANAH–YOM KIPPUR REMINDERS

The Jewish calendar includes several new year celebrations. Pesach commemorates the new year. Tu Bishevat celebrates the new year of the trees. Rosh Hashanah is the spiritual new year. The calendar dates from this holy day, Tishri being the first month.

This new year is known by several names:

YOM TERU'AH The Day of the Blowing. This refers, of course, to the shofar. The sounding of the shofar for spiritual awakening has many associations—first, the story of the sacrifice of Isaac (Genesis 20). The shofar was used in Palestine to announce the new moon, the Sabbath, holidays and other important occasions. It was the clarion call to battle. It was sounded at Mount Sinai at the time of *matan torah* (the giving of the Torah).

YOM HAZIKARON The Day of Memorial. At this season, "everything is remembered from the beginning."

YOM HADIN The Day of Judgment. At this time our deeds are evaluated and we receive the opportunity of repentance *(teshuvah)*.

THE PROPER GREETING From the evening before Rosh Hashanah until the end of Rosh Hashanah, say:
"leshanah tovah tikatevu." "May you be inscribed for a happy year."
"gam atem." "The same to you."
From the end of Rosh Hashanah until Hoshanah Rabba, say:
"gemar hatimah tovah." "May the good judgment be confirmed."

ERUV TAVSHILIN Food to be served during Rosh Hashanah may be prepared on the holiday. When Rosh Hashanah overlaps the Sabbath, food for the Sabbath may be prepared on the holiday, provided its preparation has begun before the yom tov. The first step of this preparation is called *eruv tavshilin*. A special blessing (page 244) is recited over a small quantity of cooked food (such as meat, fish or egg) and some bread shortly before the holiday begins.

ON YOM KIPPUR eve, those who have to leave their homes before it is time to light the candles (in order to reach the synagogue in time for Kol Nidre) should make arrangements to light candles at the synagogue.

MANY WOMEN wear some white article on Yom Kippur.

IT IS NOT OBLIGATORY for sick people or pregnant women to fast.

GIRLS UNDER TWELVE and boys under thirteen need not fast all day. Younger children may be given lighter meals than usual, to give them the feeling of participating in the fast.

MANY PEOPLE visit the graves of their dear ones at this season.

TASHLIH After *minhah* (afternoon service) on Rosh Hashanah (the first day unless it is the Sabbath), very pious Jews go to the banks of a river or some other body of fresh water near their homes to perform the *tashlih* ceremony in which they recite special prayers, and then shake their garments to indicate that it is within the individual's power to shake himself free of wrongdoing.

THE SHOFAR never blows on the Sabbath.

YOM KIPPUR never falls on a Friday or Sunday.

ꙮ GIFTS OF THE SEASON

Although flowers, honey cakes, candies or fruits are lovely gifts at this time, a thoughtful practical holiday memento like a hallah cloth, a divided dish for the apples and honey, sweets from Israel, a book or a ceremonial object will be a welcome change.

DO reserve your seats for the holiday services early.

Send New Year's greetings in plenty of time. Beautiful, appropriate ones can be found, including some with charming reproductions of paintings by American and Israeli artists. Check with your Sisterhood book or gift shop. Some organizations and congregations list New Year greetings in their bulletins.

Arrange all marketing, cooking and other preparations well in advance of the Holy Days.

Buy or bake the *hallot* appropriate to these festivals. Instead of the usual twisted hallah, there are the following shapes:

1. like ladders—symbolic of the hope that our prayers will reach heaven
2. like wings—suggesting that man is compared to angels
3. round—suggesting the crown of the kingdom of God.

Provide a new fruit of the season for the meal of the second night of Rosh Hashanah, such as an avocado, pomegranate, persimmon, or other fruit not usually eaten by the family. The *sheheheyanu* benediction (p. 243) is made over this.

Serve fish at the midday meal of Erev Yom Kippur as a symbol of fruitfulness and plenty.

Serve cakes and sweet refreshments during the holidays, as a reminder of the wish for a sweet year ahead.

Make a Kol Nidre offering. Many congregations and organizations send letters asking for contributions.

Have on hand the Mahzor used by your synagogue so that you can follow the service in unison.

Make appropriate arrangements for your children during the holidays. Older children should have seats reserved for them with the adults; younger children attend children's services. Families with infants or very little children should arrange for a baby sitter in advance. When the mother has to leave the synagogue at certain intervals, she should do so with minimum disturbance, quietly and courteously.

Be sure that you and your family conduct yourselves at all times in keeping with the sanctity of these Holy Days.

Make Yom Kippur a day of reverence and quiet. Boisterous merriment or riotous festivity are out of order.

Try to ascertain the time when the shofar sounds so that the children will be present.

Try to remain in the synagogue throughout the day. Be sure to be present at key prayers like *unetaneh tokef* and *kedushah,* touching and poetic outbursts that are hallowed through generations.

Urge your children not to walk in and out to visit you during services.

Stay at services through the very end. Show the proper respect.

DON'T arrange weddings or banquets during these ten days.

Don't carry your prayer book in newspaper or a paper bag.

Don't visit friends during services.

Don't congregate outside the synagogue.

Don't leave after *ne'ilah* on Yom Kippur. The entire service does not conclude until after *havdallah.*

BASIC HOLY DAY MENUS

(Recipes for dishes marked with an asterisk are given in Chapter 17.)

ROSH HASHANAH EVE

Apple Segments and Honey
Fruit Cocktail
Chicken Soup with Mandlen or Kreplach *
Roast Chicken
or
Roast Beef
Vegetable **Rice Ring**
Salad
Sweet Dessert
Tea and Honey Cake *

TO BREAK THE FAST

(Often this is a very light meal, almost like a breakfast)

(Suggestion)

Orange Juice
Eggs **Cheeses** **Cold Fish** **Salad**
Cake
Coffee

CHAPTER 8

Holy Days & Holidays II

SUKKOT, PESACH, SHAVUOT

"The Lord shall bless thee . . . in all the work of thy hands, and thou shalt be altogether joyful" (Deuteronomy 16:15)

8

Sukkot

"And thou shalt rejoice in thy festival"
(Deuteronomy 16:14)

SCARCELY ARE THE HIGH HOLY DAYS OVER when one of the year's three Festivals arrives. Sukkot comes only five days after Yom Kippur. It makes the calendar seem rather crowded; but Sukkot does provide a welcome change of mood. To be sure, you will have menus to think of, but they will be like those for any Sabbath or yom tov meals. As for the job of building the sukkah, that should be delegated to the menfolk, while the decoration of the sukkah is rightfully the children's job.

OF NATURE AND HISTORY

THIS BEAUTIFUL FESTIVAL reveals its meaning not only in the symbols which accompany its observance, but also in the names by which it is known. Both history and nature play a role here. The sukkah is a temporary booth or tabernacle of historical significance, erected to remind us of the journey our ancestors took through the wilderness, when "I did cause the children of Israel to dwell in huts" (Leviticus 23:43). But Sukkot is also called *hag ha'asif*—the Festival of Harvest—and celebrates the bounties of nature, with thanksgiving for the fruit of the soil.

Both meanings are combined in the third name—*zeman simhatenu,* or Time of Rejoicing. Joyous thanksgiving comes from the faith that it is Divine Providence which gives us our crops in the endless round of the seasons, and which enabled our ancestors to survive the trials of history. You will find this double background of nature and history present also in the other two pilgrim Festivals, Pesach and Shavuot.

A WEEK OF THANKSGIVING

SUKKOT IS A LONG HOLIDAY, beginning on the fifteenth of Tishri and lasting through the twenty-third—nine whole days. But it is subdivided. The first two days are "Sabbaths"—full holy days; the next five days are semi-holidays, called *ḥol hamo'ed,* or "weekdays of the Festival." The last of these five days, called Hoshanah Rabba, has its own observances. Finally, the eighth and ninth days of Sukkot, called Shemini Atzeret and Simhat Torah, become full holy days again. They are considered a distinct festival. The symbols of Sukkot have been put aside, but these days are still part of *zeman simḥatenu,* a sort of grand finale to the holy season.

THE SUKKAH   The most dramatic feature of this festival is the sukkah—building it, decorating it, eating the festive meals in it, lighting the yom tov candles in it, singing the kiddush and the grace in it. If it is at all possible, every family should make its own sukkah. If not (apartment dwellers do have a problem!), the family might help build or decorate the synagogue's sukkah. At the very least, everyone can visit a sukkah and partake of some refreshment in it. Most synagogues offer kiddush in the sukkah after services, so that each worshipper can recite the appropriate *beraḥah.*

But just think of the religiously creative fun the whole family can have when it builds its own sukkah! For the children particularly it adds meaning and color to the festival, so be sure that each member of the family has a share in the work. See page 102 for helpful suggestions in executing this do-it-yourself project.

If you do make a sukkah, be sure it is big enough to hold a table at which the family can sit. Then, weather permitting, meals should be served in the sukkah. Mother lights the candles there on the first two evenings, as well as on the eve of the intermediate Sabbath. A festive meal in the sukkah, in the glow of the candles, accompanied by joyful song, is a beautiful and unforgettable experience.

LULAV AND ETROG   *". . . the fruit of goodly trees"* (Leviticus
23.40) The other principal symbols of Sukkot are striking reminders of its agricultural background. The *lulav* is a palm branch
to which have been bound sprigs of myrtle and branches of the
willow tree. The *etrog* is a citron, a fragrant golden fruit which
grows in the land of Israel. A small ceremony is performed each
morning of the first seven days—either at home or in the synagogue. The *lulav* is held in the right hand, the *etrog* in the left.
As the four "species" are brought close together, a special *berahah*
is recited (the *sheheheyanu* is added on the first day). Then the entire "bouquet" is waved in the four directions of the compass. This
ceremony is omitted on a day that coincides with the Sabbath.

A host of meaningful interpretations have been attached to these
growing things. One version declares that they symbolize the human body—the oval citron, the heart; the upright palm, the spine;
the elliptical myrtle leaf, the eye; the longer willow leaf, the
mouth. The symbols indicate that we should serve God with every
fiber of our being.

IN HOME AND SYNAGOGUE   You already know how to prepare your home for this festival—the same as for Rosh Hashanah or
any festival. While cooking is permitted on yom tov, it is well to
do as much as possible in advance, so that you will be free to enjoy the holiday with your family, and to attend the synagogue
services. The greeting on a holiday is simply "Good yom tov."
Sephardic Jews say *"mo'adim le'simhah,"* a phrase also favored on
the holiday issues of Israel postage stamps. One hears increasingly
the modern Hebrew festival greeting *"hag same'ah,"* ("Happy holiday").

In the synagogue, the *lulav* and *etrog* figure prominently, so
be sure your husband takes his along (but not on the Sabbath
of Sukkot!). They are held in the hands during the chanting of
Hallel, the psalms of praise recited on festive days (Psalms 113
to 118 inclusive). Then, towards the end of the service, a colorful
procession forms of all those who have a *lulav* and *etrog*. The
procession marches around the synagogue, while the congregation
sings the *hoshana* (Save Now) poems. (*Hoshana* is the origin of
the English word "hosanna.")

HOL HAMO'ED   Life resumes its normal course during the
middle days of the festival, *hol hamo'ed*. The third to the seventh

days of Sukkot (in Israel, they also consider the second day *hol hamo'ed*), will find your children back at school, your husband back at work. But the festive mood persists; the blessing of the *lulav* and *etrog* still forms part of the morning prayers; and if you have a sukkah and the weather stays fine, it is still appropriate to eat in it.

On the Sabbath of *hol hamo'ed*, the Biblical book *Kohelet* (Ecclesiastes) is added to the scriptural lesson. When the festival begins on a Saturday, the book is read on the eighth day.

HOSHANA RABBAH   The last day of *hol hamo'ed* is called Hoshana Rabbah. It acts as a sort of aftermath of Yom Kippur. There are seven processions in the synagogue with the *lulav* and *etrog*, and then they are put away for good. The willow twigs (popularly called "hoshanas") are beaten lightly by the worshippers.

SHEMINI ATZERET   The eighth day has a double personality. Although called "shemini" (the eighth), it is also reckoned as a separate festival, and called by its own name. Meals are no longer taken in the sukkah; the *lulav* and *etrog* are not used.

A note of solemnity, a sort of counterpoint to the main theme of this "Festival of Rejoicing," is sounded more clearly on this eighth day. The service includes yizkor, memorial prayer for the departed. In addition, the solemn prayer called *geshem* (rain) is added to the *musaf* service, for at this time of year the rainy season is due to begin in the land of Israel, where the crops depend heavily on an abundance of rainfall. In most synagogues, the cantor is attired in white for this portion of the service; the traditional melodies, too, are strongly reminiscent of the Yom Kippur mood.

SIMHAT TORAH   The ninth and last day was originally just the second day of Shemini Atzeret, and is still so called in the prayer book. But Jewish communities outside Israel long ago gave it a character and name all its own—Simhat Torah, "Rejoicing in the Torah." On this day, the year-long cycle of weekly Torah readings is formally concluded with the last two chapters of Deuteronomy, and the annual round is started again from Genesis (*bereshit*—"in the beginning").

This provides the occasion for one of the most colorful synagogue ceremonies of the year. All the Torah scrolls are taken from the Ark and carried in procession (*hakafot*) around the synagogue

seven times or more, depending on the number of worshippers, each of whom is given a chance to participate. In addition, the children customarily join the procession, carrying flags which usually bear a Torah motif, and joining in the songs. A mood of jollity prevails, equalled only by the gaiety of Purim. To add to the merriment, each child is usually given candy or sweet fruit after the service. "The commandments of the Lord . . . are sweeter than honey" (Psalm 19:11).

A very special honor is awarded to two members of the congregation on Simhat Torah. The one called on to read the concluding paragraph of the Torah is referred to as *hatan torah*, while he who reads the opening paragraphs of Genesis is called *hatan bereshit*. In many congregations these gentlemen stand treat for the kiddush after the service.

This festival period has deep overtones not only for the Jewish people but for other Americans as well. In fact, Thanksgiving Day, eagerly anticipated and enthusiastically observed by all Americans, was directly inspired by Sukkot. The Pilgrims quoted the Bible when, with thankful hearts, they celebrated their first Thanksgiving Day.

From Tishri first to Tishri twenty-third, the days bring varying themes to the fore—penitence and thanksgiving, brotherhood and Jewish loyalty, solemnity and merriment, the lessons of history and the bounties of nature. So ends a sacred season which occupies most of the first three weeks of the Jewish year.

❧ HOW TO MAKE A SUKKAH

The essential characteristic of a sukkah is its roof, which must be of a temporary nature. It must have a minimum of three walls, which need not be temporary, and a clearly defined entrance. A family planning conference can be great fun; it should have the following agenda:

LOCATION. Try to use existing structures. The garage, an outside wall of the house—these can provide ready-made walls. If a fence or wall joins your house at right angles, so much the better; that gives you two sides to start with. Be sure the space is big enough to contain table and chairs, and that the location opens to the sky—not under a tree or porch. A secondary factor, but one worth considering, is nearness to the kitchen, so that food can be carried out easily.

THE WALLS. These may be made of lumber, plywood, or even canvas. Old doors are usually not particularly attractive, but they may serve as part of a wall. In any case, the structure must be strong enough to withstand the wind—another reason for utilizing at least one existing wall.

THE ROOF. The best way to make your temporary roof is to lay long laths or strips of wood, about two or three inches wide, from wall to wall, and to place your covering material crosswise on this base. Lay your laths in both directions to form a lattice if you think your thatching needs stronger support. The covering material itself (called *sehah*) must be fashioned from plants in their natural state as they grew from the soil—reeds, rushes, bamboo shoots, evergreen branches. Do not tie them together. They must be thick enough so that more shade than sun finds its way into the sukkah, but thin enough so that you can "see the stars."

THE ENTRANCE. A door is unnecessary. A curtain, drape or the like will serve the purpose.

THE FLOOR. An old rug or mat makes a satisfactory floor covering.

DECORATION. Autumn fruits, vegetables and gourds, can be hung from the roof. Clusters of grapes, red apples, eggplants, squashes and peppers all add color. Try to get very small eggplants and squashes, tiny pumpkins, and the long Italian red peppers. Tie a string to the stem of each and tack this to the boards of the roof. Fruit and vegetables may also be hung on the walls. Children love to string cranberries for decoration. The walls may be painted with murals of the holiday theme, and pictures may be hung. Flowers add a festive touch to the sukkah.

SUKKOT SUGGESTIONS

A mobile fashioned of Sukkot symbols or fruit makes a handsome decoration for your sukkah or living room.

A special container for the *etrog* is nice to have. Boxes made for this purpose range from simple inexpensive items to beautiful creations of great artistry. With a little searching and imagination, you might find an old silver candy box, sugar container or jewelry case which can be converted to an *etrog* box and suitably engraved. Making an *etrog* box out of wood, basketry or metal could be a children's craft project.

You may wonder what to do with the *etrog* after the holiday. If you can accumulate enough *etrogim* from your friends, you can make an exotic jam or preserve (see Chapter 17). If not, put your own among your linens; like lavender, it gives a pleasant aroma that lingers for months.

Use short candles in the sukkah so that they will burn out by the time the evening meal is over. Long candles could be a fire hazard.

If your husband is honored with *ḥatan torah* or *ḥatan bereshit,* arrange a small kiddush for the congregation to show your appreciation.

You might start a "tour of Sukkot" in your community.

Suggest to your Sisterhood, or other women's organizations, that it sponsor a contest for the most attractive miniature sukkah or table centerpiece. Tinkertoys, Minibricks or toy logs form suitable materials for these.

If you live in an apartment house, join with a group of other tenants in asking the landlord's permission to build a sukkah on the roof.

❧ GIFTS OF THE SEASON

An *etrog* box, a basket of fruit, or the book of *Kohelet* make appropriate gifts.

DO take the first step toward the building of your sukkah on Yom Kippur night, even if it means only hammering in the first nail.

Offer to help decorate the congregational sukkah.

Get your own *etrog* and *lulav.* They can usually be ordered through your synagogue.

Scout vegetable markets for squashes, eggplants, peppers, Indian corn, cranberries, and other autumn fruits and vegetables that will not deteriorate during the week as they hang in the sukkah.

Invite guests into the sukkah. You might include your children's playmates and school friends, and your non-Jewish neighbors.

See that your children take part in the Simḥat Torah procession. Provide them with flags and apples if your synagogue does not do this.

Check the time schedule for *hakafot* so that the youngsters' mealtime and bedtime can be arranged accordingly.

Plan to read the book of *Kohelet* during the holiday.

DON'T handle the *etrog* carelessly—the *pittum* (a knob at the tip) breaks off easily, making it unfit to use.

Don't recite the blessing for the *lulav* and *etrog* on Shabbat.

Don't let the week pass without visiting a sukkah.

❧ A SUKKOT TEA

CENTERPIECE SUGGESTIONS

Cornucopias with fruit or flowers.

A miniature sukkah with miniature table and chairs, candlesticks, with little birthday candles, food. A small doll house with a removable roof can serve as the sukkah. Your children will enjoy lending their toys for this.

The lulav and etrog.

INVITATIONS OR PLACE CARDS

Cards decorated with Sukkot designs and symbols.

Cards in the shape of the sukkah.

Miniature etrog made of yellow jelly beans and lulav made of bits of green plants pasted on cards.

REFRESHMENTS

(Recipes for dishes marked with an asterisk are given in Chapter 17.)

Punch

Fruit Bowl

Strudel °

Assorted Cakes and Cookies

Tea and Coffee

Pesach

*"Let every person, in every generation, think of himself as
a former slave, freed from bondage in Egypt"*
(Haggadah)

THAT ANY PEOPLE should commemorate their descent from
slaves, as we Jews do when we celebrate the springtime
festival of Pesach (Passover), must seem remarkable. The
fact is that the Exodus from Egypt marked the birth of the Jewish
people, and this is proudly proclaimed not only at Passover, the
"season of our freedom," but in the prayers of every day of the year
and in the kiddush of every Sabbath and Festival. The Torah says
repeatedly, "Remember, you were slaves in Egypt"—and the Jew
has remembered.

On Pesach, he recalls the story of the wandering in the desert
for forty years, of Moses' acceptance of the Torah on Mount Sinai,
of the entrance into the Promised Land. The dramatic story is in
the Book of Exodus. The story is also retold, with commentary, in
the Haggadah, the guide book to Pesach.

NAMES OF THE FESTIVAL

IN ENGLISH, the holiday is called Passover. (During the final plague,
the Angel of Death "passed over" the houses of the Israelites when
he smote the first-born of the Egyptians.) It is also called:

ḤAG ḤAMATZOT—Feast of Unleavened Bread
ZEMAN ḤERUTENU—Season of Our Freedom

The holiday is agricultural as well as historical in origin. Spring was the time of the barley harvest in Palestine.

This inspiring festival, commencing on Nisan fifteenth and lasting eight days, is unique in a number of ways. Its principal ceremony, the family Seder, belongs to the home rather than the synagogue; its effect on the household is greatest because of the special Passover food requirements (the absence of leaven). And so the preparations for this festival are more elaborate than any other.

GETTING READY

SPRING HAS MANY poetic associations of romance and rebirth. For the homemaker, however, it used to be a time of hard work. It meant spring cleaning with its rug beating, curtain stretching and general household upheaval. For the Jewish housewife, it meant all this plus the complicated preparation for Pesach. Such spring cleaning as is necessary is done not solely for sanitary reasons but as a part of the religious ritual tied up with a great epochal event.

Today, just as spring cleaning has been simplified by modern appliances, so Pesach preparation has been made less arduous. Even cooking and baking are less of a chore; freezers make it possible to do much in advance, and a variety of Passover foods make their appearance on the market.

Time-saving devices, unfortunately, are sometimes handicaps to the creative participation of the children and the family. It is wise, even in a household where there is help, to allow the children to bring up the Passover dishes, to prepare the horseradish, to make the ḥaroset, and to assist in setting the table. The children delight in recognizing the almost-forgotten pattern of last year's Pesach dishes, in identifying the salt-water dish, in unpacking the matzah cover.

Though careful preparations go into making this holiday meaningful, ingenuity need not be taxed, because the basic order has been prescribed. Seder, the familiar term for the festive meal, actually means "order."

After the marketing has been done, the house cleaned, the cabinets newly lined, utensils are "kashered" (p 110) and put in their place. The night before the eve of Passover, the father performs the *bedikat ḥametz* (search for leaven, p. 109).

Then Pesach proceeds like all other festivals. On the first two nights, Mother lights the candles with the appropriate benediction (p. 239), preceding the Seder.

THE SEDER

Tʜᴇ sᴇᴅᴇʀ is the most impressive family meal of the year. It is enhanced by a beautifully set table and by specially invited relatives and other guests. Family melodies, the children's eager voices asking the "four questions"—plus many of their own— enrich the occasion. It is given religious and spiritual significance by the intriguing symbols on the table.

Tʜᴇ Sʏᴍʙᴏʟs   While some individuals and nations tend to forget their humble origins, we remind ourselves annually that we were once slaves. Tangible symbols on the Seder table help even the youngest child understand the principles of freedom. These symbols are:

ᴍᴀᴛᴢᴏᴛ. Three whole *matzot* (unleavened bread), placed between three napkins or in a specially sectioned cover. This reminds us of the bread made in haste by the Israelite women on their hurried departure from Egypt. The three *matzot* also represent the three traditional groups of Jews—Kohen, Levi and Yisrael.

A large plate on which are set:

ʀᴏᴀsᴛᴇᴅ ʙᴏɴᴇ *(zero'a)*. Remembrance of the sacrificial lamb offered by the Israelites, and eaten on the eve of their departure from Egypt.

ʀᴏᴀsᴛᴇᴅ ᴇɢɢ *(beitzah)*. Recalls the individual festival offering of Temple days, known as the *hagigah*.

ᴍᴏʀᴏʀ. Bitter herbs (horseradish is usually used) as a reminder of the bitterness of the bondage in Egypt.

ᴋᴀʀᴘᴀs. Celery or parsley or any other green vegetable suggests the first green of spring. It is also said to represent a first course in the meal, which in ancient times only free men could enjoy.

sᴀʟᴛ ᴡᴀᴛᴇʀ. Into which the greens are dipped, described as the tears shed for suffering and persecution.

ʜᴀʀᴏsᴇᴛ. A mixture of chopped apples and nuts, cinnamon and wine, suggesting the bricks that the Israelites made for Pharaoh.

In addition to a wine cup for each member of the family:

CUP OF ELIJAH. An especially attractive wine goblet is placed on the table as an extra cup. According to legend, the prophet Elijah may unexpectedly arrive to drink from that cup. He is the messenger of the Messiah who will someday bring peace and freedom to all the world.

The symbols may be placed on any large plate. A special divided seder plate adds dignity and beauty to the table. The symbols and the ceremonies related to them are outlined in the Haggadah.

THE HAGGADAH   Haggadah means "recital." It tells the story of freedom with appropriate prayers and praise, and includes anecdotes, tales, references to great historic episodes in Jewish history, and special songs to keep the children awake through the long service. The Seder is enhanced if you have handsome illustrated Haggadahs with interesting commentaries. This leads to stimulating discussions during the meal, bringing the group closer to the idea of *kol hamarbeh:* that anyone who expands the retelling of the story of freedom is praiseworthy.

ORDER OF THE SEDER SERVICE

Kiddush, as on other festival evenings
Washing of the hands without the customary blessing
Eating of the greens dipped in salt water
Breaking of the middle cake of matzah; putting half away for the
    afikoman
Recital of the Haggadah
Washing of the hands with the customary blessing
Blessing for bread over the topmost matzah
Dividing the topmost matzah among those at the table
Eating of the bitter herb dipped in *haroset*
Eating of the bitter herb with *matzot*
The Passover meal
Eating of the *afikoman*
Grace after the meal
Chanting of the Hallel
Closing prayer

SYNAGOGUE SERVICES

Yom tov services are held on the evenings of the holiday before sundown, usually attended by the men and boys. The family attends morning holiday services on the first and last two days. (The days in between are *hol hamo'ed*—semi-holidays.) On the first day of the festival, a special prayer for *tal* (dew) is chanted. In this prayer, Jews all over the world pray that there will be plenty of dew in Israel during the dry summer months when no rain falls. On the second day, the counting of the *omer* is begun.

If one of the days of *hol hamo'ed* occurs on the Sabbath, it is customary to read the Song of Songs, one of the most poetic books of the Bible. The Sabbath preceding Passover is known as Shabbat Hagadol, the "Great Sabbath."

FESTIVAL OF FREEDOM

Pharaoh has been a symbol of tyrants who have emerged from time to time in different parts of the world. Passover is a constant reminder that present-day dictators, too, must ultimately be overthrown.

"And ye shall proclaim liberty throughout the land." These ringing words from Leviticus (25:10) are engraved on the historic Liberty Bell which hangs in Philadelphia, and they come down to us at the Passover season to reaffirm our belief in liberty, democracy and civil rights for all.

PASSOVER PARTICULARS

❧ PREPARATION

The essential feature of Passover preparation requires the elimination of all *ḥametz* (leaven) from the home. This is done by actually removing any of the proscribed foods (page 112), by changing dishes that have been used during the rest of the year, and by "kashering" (ritual cleansing) of certain kinds of utensils (page 110). It is also done in the symbolic ceremony of *bedikat ḥametz*.

BEDIKAT ḤAMETZ (SEARCH FOR LEAVEN) The night before the eve of Passover, a formal search for leaven begins immediately after nightfall. The man of the house "hides" some *ḥametz*—usually a few bread crumbs

—in an obvious place, perhaps on a window sill. Later, carrying a wooden spoon, a feather, and a lighted candle, he searches every nook and cranny to be sure no leaven is left. (He may be accompanied by a child or other member of the family.) When he comes to the previously deposited crumbs, he carefully sweeps them up with the feather into the spoon, saying a special blessing found in the Haggadah. The crumbs, together with the spoon and feathers, are burned before eleven o'clock on the next morning.

When the first day of Passover falls on a Sunday, the *bedikat ḥametz* ceremony is performed on the preceding Thursday, in order to avoid its taking place on the Sabbath.

ERUV TAVSHILIN Matzah is substituted for the bread (see page 91).

"KASHERING" DISHES AND UTENSILS Special dishes are stored to be used only on Passover. Certain utensils used during the year, however, may be made kosher for Pesach use through a special process of "kashering." This may be effected either by glowing or purging, or, in the case of glassware, by immersion.

GLOWING The object is heated red hot till it emits sparks. Utensils such as frying pans are "kashered" by glowing, since they can come in direct contact with the fire.

PURGING The object is placed in boiling water for a minute. The water should overflow, and a small piece of red-hot iron placed in the water hastens this process. Silver or other metal cutlery and tableware that is flat and of one piece may be purged by this method. Metal objects used for cooking *only* but *not* for baking may be "kashered" for Pesach.

IMMERSION Glassware should be immersed and covered with fresh cold water for three days. The water is changed each day shortly before nightfall.

✥ SPECIAL NOTES

1. No object may be "kashered" unless twenty-four hours have passed since it was last used for leaven.

2. Dishes of earthenware, wood, agate, plastic, porcelain, enamel or any absorbent material cannot be "kashered" for Passover use.

3. Objects that cannot be thoroughly cleansed, such as a grater or sieve or narrow-necked bottle, may not be processed for Passover use.

5. All covers must be included in the ritual cleansing.

6. Utensils used for baking during the year may not be used for Pesach.

7. Consult your rabbi when in doubt.

KITCHEN EQUIPMENT

THE STOVE is prepared by scrubbing and cleansing all parts and then turning on a full flame in the oven, the broiler and all burners.

THE REFRIGERATOR is thoroughly scrubbed and cleansed after all *hametz* is removed.

NOTE: Aluminum foil can be used to line the burner grids, the inside of the oven and the oven tray; the refrigerator shelves; and for covering kitchen counters and all work surfaces.

THE FREEZER. This wonderful invention makes it possible for you to prepare some of the holiday food in advance. The freezer should be emptied and thoroughly cleansed before any Passover foods are placed in it. Then fish for "gefillte" fish can be purchased when it is economical and stored in the freezer. Cakes can be baked a week or so in advance, packed well and stored. Of course, provision must be made in advance for the stove to be properly cleansed and an area cleared for Passover preparation.

FOOD STORAGE. Passover staples should be ordered several days in advance and placed in some specially allotted section of the house away from household traffic.

FOODS FOR PESACH

❧ PERMITTED

The following items do not require a "Kosher L'Pesach" label if they are in *unopened* packages or containers.

Salt	Sugar
Pepper	Tea

Vegetables (except peas and beans; stringbeans permitted). Fruits and vegetables normally permitted for Passover use are permitted in their frozen state.

If rabbinical authority indicates that the following items of food have been manufactured and wrapped free from contact with *hametz* and are certified as fit for Passover use (please turn page):

Beverages
Butter
Cakes
Canned goods
Candies
Cheese
Coffee (but not "instant")
Dried fruits
Jams and jellies
Liquors
Matzah

Matzah flour
Milk
Passover noodles
Processed foods
Relishes
Salad oils
Shortenings
Vegetable gelatins
Vinegars
Wines

NOTE: *Labels and tags marked "Kosher L'Pesach" are of no value unless they bear rabbinical signature. This statement also applies to products manufactured in Israel.*

❧ PROHIBITED

Barley
Biscuits
Cakes
Cereals
Crackers
Dried beans
Dried peas
Hops

Leavened bread
Oats
Rice
Rye
Wheat
All liquids which contain in-
    gredients or flavors made
    from grain alcohol

MORE PARTICULARS

❧ TA'ANIT BEHORIM

The fourteenth day of Nisan is *ta'anit behorim,* Fast of the First-born. Because God spared the firstborn of the Israelites during the plague in Egypt, the eldest son in a family is required to fast on the day before Passover. However, participation in a *siyyum* (completing a unit of learning) exempts the firstborn from fasting. Therefore, the custom arose of inviting the eldest sons of the community to such a *siyyum* the day before Passover.

❧ MA'OT HITTIM

The community funds raised for the provision of *matzot* and other holiday requisites for those requiring financial assistance are called *ma'ot hittim* (money for wheat). In ancient days the major purchase was wheat for *matzot*.

💥 GIFTS OF THE SEASON

Appropriate gifts for Passover include a Seder plate, a wine cup, a handsome silver Cup of Elijah, a *matzot* cover, a dish for salt water, *mayyim aharonim* (for washing the hands at the table before the grace), or an illustrated Haggadah.

DO start your preparations early enough.

Make the house sparkling clean, and your table as beautiful as possible.

Invite as a guest someone who is far from his own home.

Have uniform Haggadahs for everyone at the table so all can participate in the Seder without difficulty. These Haggadahs are in·addition to the decorative ones, or ones of special interest.

Provide or make a three-sectioned cover for the *matzot;* you might embroider or appliqué it.

Use an attractive dish for the Seder plate.

Help your husband select, in advance, sections of the Haggadah to be assigned for individual reading in English by those who may not be able to follow the Hebrew.

Rehearse *mah nishtanah* with the child who will ask the four questions.

Place a saucer under each wine cup to prevent excessive stains on the tablecloth.

Arrange a cushion or pillow for the master of the house to recline on during the meal, in the style of the "freemen" in ancient times.

Provide an appropriate small reward for the child who finds the *afikoman*. During the Seder, the father hides a part of the middle matzah to be distributed and eaten later by all present. Toward the end of the meal, the father pretends not to notice that the children hide it. He offers a reward for its return, since the meal cannot be properly concluded until each person has tasted a piece of the *afikoman*.

Suggest that one of the children prepare a talk for the Seder on freedom in modern times. A token gift can be given in appreciation.

"Dress" for the Seder.

DON'T rush through the Seder just to get it over with.

Don't use miscellaneous makeshift dishes for Pesach; an attractive inexpensive set used annually for the holiday adds to its beauty and dignity.

Don't deprive your family of the joy and fun of "making Pesach" by going to a resort for the holidays.

❧ SUGGESTION FOR A SEDER MENU

These suggestions are in addition to the ceremonial foods. Recipes for dishes with an asterisk (and also for *haroset*) will be found in Chapter 17.

Hard Boiled Eggs in Salt Water

Fruit Cup

Gefillte Fish *

Chicken Soup with K'naidlach *

Roast Turkey

Passover Potato Kugel *   Candied Carrots

Green Salad

Strawberry Delight *   Passover Spongecake *

Tea or Black Coffee

Shavuot

*"[The Torah] is a tree of life and happy are those who
guide themselves by it" (Proverbs 3:18)*

G O TO THE WOMEN FIRST," Moses was told by God. "Acquaint
them with the principles of Judaism. They will accept
them; then the men will follow." This Midrash wisely
recognizes that the woman sets the pattern of learning for her
family.

Shavuot celebrates the birthday of our religion, just as Rosh
Hashanah celebrates the birthday of mankind and Pesach sym-
bolizes the birthday or independence of the Jewish people.
Shavuot is pictured as the day when Israel was wedded to God,
just as Passover is described as the betrothal of Israel and God.

Shavuot makes us keenly aware that it is principally in the
home that the Ten Commandments must be stressed. By the emphasis on honoring Father and Mother, by the observance of a
day of rest, by her social conduct, and finally through the inculca-
tion of the love of God, the woman sets the moral example. In the
kitchen, in the living room, in the bedroom, her standard for ethical Jewish living influences the family.

NAMES OF THE HOLIDAY

SHAVUOT FALLS on the sixth and seventh of Sivan. Like some of the other festivals, it has more than one name. It is called:

SHAVUOT—the Feast of Weeks, from the Hebrew word for "weeks," since it comes seven weeks or fifty days after the second day of Pesach.

PENTECOST—the fiftieth day.

HAG HABIKURIM—Feast of the First Fruits.

ZEMAN MATAN TORATENU—Season of the Giving of the Torah (the Ten Commandments).

A LOVELY SEASON

SHAVUOT IS CELEBRATED with seriousness and dignity. It comes at a lovely season in our part of the world, late May or early June. It is easy, therefore, to find greens, flowers and plants to decorate the home and synagogue to suggest the agricultural nature of the festival.

HOLIDAY EVE On the eve of the festival, the men and boys go to the synagogue for the *ma'ariv* service, while the woman of the house lights the candles at home with the appropriate blessings (page 238). After services, the evening meal follows the festive pattern of other holiday meals with the kiddush, *motzi* and grace. It is customary to serve dairy foods on Shavuot.

THE SYNAGOGUE SERVICE Yom tov services are held in the synagogue. On the morning of the second day, yizkor (memorial service) is read. Torah is emphasized throughout the services in poems and prayers. The Ten Commandments are recited; the Book of Ruth is read.

THE BOOK OF RUTH

THE CLASSIC PASTORAL IDYLL depicted in the Book of Ruth gives the woman still another identification with this holiday. The reading of this scroll is appropriate from two points of view—the story takes place in ancient Palestine during the harvest festival, and Ruth accepts Judaism and the laws of the Torah.

Even though history considers Ruth the heroine of the story, it is important for women to note that it was Naomi, her mother-in-law, who inspired her. When you read the story, you will see that Naomi, bereft of her husband and sons, alone and poor, prepares to return to her homeland, Palestine. Ruth, her son's widow, a Moabite, surrounded by her own people in a land of plenty, implores her mother-in-law, "Entreat me not to leave thee . . . for whither thou goest, I will go; and where thou lodgest, I will lodge; thy people shall be my people, and thy god, my God" (Ruth 1:16). Naomi must have been a woman of rare understanding, gentleness and moral character to influence a beautiful young girl of another religion, with whom she no longer had any ties, to follow her and accept her fate and her faith.

CONFIRMATION AND CONSECRATION

REFORM JUDAISM introduced the custom of confirmation on this holiday. This ceremony, in which boys and girls publicly pledge themselves to lead lives based on the Torah, has been accepted by many Conservative synagogues.

More recently, and perhaps more significantly, some synagogues have initiated the custom of asking young children preparing to enter Hebrew school to participate in the Shavuot services. The children take part in a ceremony of consecration to the Torah and Jewish study.

Because the Ten Commandments are almost universally accepted, this holiday has tremendous significance, not only for the Jewish people but for all mankind.

SHAVUOT SPECIALS

THIS SEASON is an appropriate time for you and your family to register for a Hebrew class, a Bible study group or a similar course for the coming fall.

THE TRADITION of organizing the menfolk to stay up all night on Shavuot studying the Torah is an old one. It has been suggested that the custom of serving milk foods on this holiday started with the serving of coffee and cake to those who stayed up late to study.

IN ISRAEL TODAY, the custom of bringing the first fruits—*bikurim*—has been reintroduced in the form of kibbutz harvest festivities and community celebrations. Children wear garlands in gay processions through the streets.

THE TEN COMMANDMENTS
(Exodus 20:2-14)

א   I am the Lord thy God.

ב   Thou shalt have no other gods before Me.

ג   Thou shalt not take the name of the Lord thy God in vain.

ד   Remember the Sabbath day to keep it holy.

ה   Honor thy father and thy mother.

ו   Thou shalt not murder.

ז   Thou shalt not commit adultery.

ח   Thou shalt not steal.

ט — Thou shalt not bear false witness against thy neighbor.

י   Thou shalt not covet.

🌱 GIFTS OF THE SEASON

A divided dish for "blintzes" and sour cream, plants, bouquets of dried flowers imported from Israel, a copy of the Book of Ruth make appropriate gifts. A unique gift is the miniature replica of the Dead Sea scrolls, available at many book and gift shops.

DO read the story of Ruth from the Bible, in English, to your family.

Provide a new fruit of the season (cherries, perhaps) over which to say *sheheheyanu* (p. 240).

Suggest to your children that they write in advance to Keren Hayesod, Youth Division, P.O.B. 583, Jerusalem, for cards on which flowers of Israel have been pressed by Israeli school children.

Arrange for the children to plant something new in your own garden or window box.

Decorate your home with flowers, leaves and plants.

Prepare dairy delicacies like blintzes, noodle pudding or cheesecake.

Plan an appropriate party if there are confirmants in your family.

Co-operate with your Sisterhood in decorating the synagogue for this holiday.

🌱 SHAVUOT CONFIRMATION PARTY

CENTERPIECE SUGGESTIONS

Arrangement of greens around a scroll.

Basket of fruits.

Sheaves of wheat (can be purchased from florist).

Miniature flowerpots set in a row.

Small books between book ends.

PLACE CARDS

Small Torah scrolls made from pieces of paper wound around toothpicks or matchsticks and tied with ribbon.

Bits of wheat attached to cards.

Cards cut in shape of Tablets of the Law.

Suggestion: The children can make garlands of fresh flowers and wear them.

PARTY MENU

(Recipes for dishes marked with an asterisk are given in Chapter 17.)

Open Face Sandwiches
Peaches and Pears Stuffed with Cream Cheese
Ice Cream Molded into Tablets   Cheesecake °
Chocolate Milk   Coffee

🌷 SHAVUOT SUPPER MENU
Schav, or Fruit Soup, or Cream Soup
Baked Fish
Noodle Cheese Kugel ° or Cheese or Cherry Blintzes °
Salad
Coffee   Cake
(The cake icing might be decorated with tablets or sheaves of wheat.)

YOU MIGHT USE THE FOLLOWING FOR REFERENCE BEFORE A PARTICULAR HOLIDAY

THE JEWISH HOME BEAUTIFUL by Betty D. Greenberg and Althea O. Silverman (Women's League). In addition to brief descriptions of the significance of the holidays, this book gives photographs of table settings, music, menus and recipes for each holiday.

THE JEWISH FESTIVALS by Hayyim Schauss (Union of American Hebrew Congregations. Also appeared under the title *Guide to the Jewish Holy Days* in a Schocken Paperback). This is a good reference for all the holidays from their beginnings to the present. It gives complete historical background as well as significance and observance.

JEWISH HOLIDAYS AND FESTIVALS by Ben M. Edidin (Hebrew Publishing Company). A clear, compact presentation of holiday significance and observance.

A TREASURY OF JEWISH HOLIDAYS by Hyman E. Goldin (Twayne Publishing Company). Gives the significance of the holidays, their celebration and the story behind each.

DAYS OF AWE by S. Y. Agnon (Schocken). Treasury of legends and traditions concerning Rosh Hashanah, Yom Kippur, and the days between.

🌿 YOUR CHILDREN MIGHT LIKE

MY JEWISH HOLIDAYS by Azriel Eisenberg and Jessie B. Robinson (United Synagogue Commission on Jewish Education). A handsome spiral-bound book full of charming illustrations. After a brief statement on the significance of each holiday, there are games, quizzes, puzzles, party ideas, all graphically presented. Also includes good suggested reading for each holiday.

JEWISH HOLIDAY PARTY BOOK by Lilliam S. Abramson and Lillian T. Leiderman (Bloch Publishing Company). A practical illustrated guide for planning parties for children aged five to twelve. Includes invitations, "what to serve" suggestions, games.

DAYS AND WAYS by Mamie G. Gamoran (Union of American Hebrew Congregations). Interesting presentation of holidays and ceremonies for the child from nine to twelve.

HOLIDAYS AROUND THE WORLD by Joseph Gaer (Little, Brown and Company). A collection of stories descriptive of festival days of all the great religions, for children from ten to fourteen. Boys and girls might like to learn about some holidays besides their own.

ADVENTURES OF K' TONTON by Sadie Rose Weilerstein (Women's League for Conservative Judaism). The adventures of a little Jewish Tom Thumb.

K'TONTON IN ISRAEL by Sadie Rose Weilerstein (Women's League for Conservative Judaism).

🌿 FOR PESACH

In addition to the uniform Haggadahs which you will have in duplicate so that the family can follow the Seder easily together, you might like to have some unusual or handsomely illustrated Haggadahs for special readings or reference. (These make fine gifts, too.) Here are a few:

HAGGADAH translated by Maurice Samuel with an introduction by Louis Finklestein (Hebrew Publishing Company).

THE PASSOVER HAGGADAH arranged and edited by Rabbi Menachem M. Kasher (American Biblical Encyclopedia Society). This comprehensive annotated edition with supplements makes a good text.

THE PASSOVER HAGGADAH commentary by E. D. Goldschmidt (Schocken). Illustrations from the famous Prague Haggadah of 1526.

THE NEW HAGGADAH edited by Mordecai M. Kaplan, Eugene Kohn, and Ira Eisenstein (Jewish Reconstructionist Foundation). An abbreviated Haggadah, good for special readings.

There are several Haggadahs, not for table use, but beautiful for display:

HAGGADAH edited by Cecil Roth and illustrated by Arthur Szyk, published in Israel. Szyk's illustrations in full color, are magnificent. The volume is bound in velvet and boxed.

PESACH HAGGADAH illuminated by Kafra (Feldheim Publishing Company). This is very handsome; in Hebrew only, with a separate supplement in English.

SARAJEVO HAGGADAH introduction by Cecil Roth (Harcourt, Brace and World). A truly unique and impressively beautiful edition.

MY HAGGADAH by Pins and Scotch (Behrman). A picture Haggadah for the very young, 3-6 years old.

THE CHILDREN'S HAGGADAH edited by Dr. A. M. Silberman (Shapiro, Valentine & Co., London). Also beautifully illustrated.

HAGGADAH, drawings by Ben Shahn, text by Cecil Roth (Houghton).

CHAPTER 9

Hanukkah and Purim

"For the wonders wrought for our fathers, in those days, at this season" (Siddur)

9

Hanukkah

"A great miracle happened there"

THE TORCH OF LIBERTY, the impressive beacon which stands
at the gateway to America, is held by a woman. On Hanukkah, the Jewish woman upholds a torch of liberty in her
own home—the eight-branched candlestick, the menorah.

FESTIVAL OF LIGHTS

HANUKKAH, THE HEBREW WORD for dedication, reminds us of the
cleansing of the Temple, and the rededication to the religious and
moral principles of Judaism. The holiday is also called the Festival
of Lights. It begins on the twenty-fifth day of Kislev, usually in
December, and continues for eight days.

THE STORY

ON THIS HOLIDAY, parents and children review the story of the
brave Maccabees who fought the Syrian-Greek tyrant Antiochus.
The story has been preserved in two books of the Apocrypha,
Maccabees I and II.

Mattathias and his five sons led the long and hard fight of the
Jews to preserve their traditions and religion despite the power

and cruelty of Antiochus and his armies. In 164 B.C.E., when Judah Maccabeus and a small, courageous band of followers recaptured Jerusalem, their first act was the cleansing of the Temple which had been defiled by the Syrians.

The Talmud tells the story of the cruse of oil. When the Maccabees came to rededicate the Temple, they found one flask with sufficient oil for only one day, but it miraculously lasted for eight days.

AT HOME

THE LAMP, called the menorah, is given a prominent place; in the evening, the family gathers around it. The father recites the benediction (page 240) while he lights the candles or oil wicks. Then all the members of the family chant the hymns *Hanerot Halalu* and *Ma'oz Tzur* (for words, see your prayer book).

There are nine places in the Hanukkah lamp—one for each night, plus the *shamash* (the work-candle), which is used to light the others. One candle is lit the first night, two the second and so on till all eight candles shine on the last night (see next page).

The lighting of the menorah is a beautiful and impressive ceremony, eagerly anticipated by the children. The evenings should be festive with gifts and games. The children delight in spinning the "dreidel." The custom of giving Hanukkah "gelt" (money), a few coins to each child, has been expanded into the exchanging of Hanukkah gifts. Young children in the family usually receive some small token on each of the eight nights. Stories are told of the origin of the holiday, and of its celebration in modern Israel. "Latkes" (potato or cheese pancakes) are often served.

School and business activities go on as usual.

IN THE SYNAGOGUE

THE SYNAGOGUE SERVICE is similar to the regular weekly service, with the addition of the lighting of the Hanukkah candles and the recitation of *al hanissim*. In this prayer we thank God for all miracles. The whole history of Hanukkah is told with Mattathias and his sons as its heroes.

IN THE COMMUNITY   Hanukkah, like Purim, is a joyous, merry

holiday. Centers, Hebrew schools, and clubs celebrate with plays, concerts and parties. Gift giving is extended to the giving of charity.

IN ISRAEL   The Israelis of today are sometimes called modern Maccabees, whose courage made possible the miracle of the Jewish state. The celebration of this holiday takes on added significance in Israel. On the first night of Hanukkah, Israelis light a torch in Modin (home of the Maccabees) and a runner carries it to scouts stationed at other points, who light their torches from the first one, and so the light is carried, relay fashion, through the land. In the kibbutzim (co-operative colonies) and in the cities, large menorahs shine from synagogue façades and watchtowers.

Kindling of lights signifies many things for us. The mother lights the candles to usher in the Shabbat and the festivals. The father lights the *havdallah* candle to say farewell to the Sabbath. An eternal light *(ner tamid)* burns unceasingly in the synagogue. A candle is lit as a "yahrzeit" lamp in memory of a departed parent.

Through the tiny flickering lights of the Hanukkah lamp, we see the panorama of Jewish history, the struggle for freedom, the victory of a weak minority over the powerful forces of tyranny, the miracle of the cruse of oil, the triumph of right over might, and especially the steadfast faith of our people in God.

HANUKKAH HIGHLIGHTS

THE MENORAH is usually made of metal, but today many other materials are effectively used. With a little investigation, you may find a beautiful old one or a handsome modern one. A well-made attractive Hanukkah lamp is a worthwhile investment. Although you use it for only eight days annually, it is a decorative object in the home throughout the year.

REMINDER: Arrange and light the candles in this traditional order: On the first evening, place the first candle at the right end of the lamp as you face it. On each succeeding evening, place one additional candle to the left (two, the second night; three, the third; and so on). Always light the newly added candle first, then light the other candles from left to right.

THE TALMUD long ago recognized that the woman might also have the privilege of lighting the Hanukkah candles.

ON FRIDAY, the Hanukkah lights are kindled before the Sabbath lights. On Saturday night, they are lit after the *havdallah* ceremony.

IF POSSIBLE, put the lighted menorah where the lights will be seen from outside the house.

OLDER CHILDREN might be given menorahs of their own.

THE NAME MACCABEE given to Judah and his followers is said to come from the initial letters of their battle slogan, *"mi kamoha ba'elim adonai?"* ("Who is like unto Thee among the mighty, O Lord?")

THE "DREIDEL" has on its four sides the four Hebrew letters *nun, gimel, hay, shin,* which stand for the words *"nes gadol hayah sham."* This means "A great miracle happened there." In Israel, since the rebirth of the state, the letter *shin* has been replaced with the letter *pay,* to signify *"nes gadol hayah po,"* "A great miracle happened *here."*

GAMES such as checkers, chess, dominoes and cards, as well as riddles and puzzles, find popular favor during Hanukkah. Though games of chance are usually frowned upon, cards and "dreidel" games have their place on this gay holiday.

✸ GIFTS OF THE SEASON

An attractive or unusual menorah makes an appropriate present. For the children, "dreidels" filled with candy are available; books and records telling the story of the Maccabees make excellent gifts.

DO prepare for the holiday by shining up the Hanukkah lamp and buying the special Hanukkah candles. Attractive varicolored ones from Israel usually can be obtained in your Sisterhood gift and book shop.

Light the candles in the presence of all the family, before the youngsters have gone to bed.

Stress the spiritual as well as the military victory of the Maccabees.

Make the week a joyous one for the children with gifts, games, special treats and songs.

Provide materials with which the children can make Hanukkah decorations and symbols, such as clay for modeling a menorah, or colored paper for making "dreidels," and thin wires and plastics for making mobiles of the Hanukkah symbols.

Look for attractive Hanukkah gift wrappings and party accessories. Many large stores feature them at this season of the year, or will order them on request. Of course, check your Sisterhood gift and book shop.

Use ingenuity in giving Hanukkah "gelt." For example, tape a few bright coins on a gift box.

Make one of the gifts to the children something of Jewish significance.

Encourage the children to participate in Hebrew school or club programs.

Serve "latkes" at least once during the holiday.

DON'T let an electric menorah take the place of the candle-lighting ceremony.

Don't rush the ceremony.

🌑 LATKE PARTY

An evening party when the candles are lit is an enjoyable way to celebrate. Neighbors, Jewish and non-Jewish alike, might be invited. You can prepare small gifts for all the children who come; let your youngsters help in making the invitations and decorations and in planning the gifts and games.

INVITATIONS

Cutouts in the shape of "dreidels" or candles.

DECORATIONS

Paper decorations in the shape of stars, candles, "dreidels," menorahs, lions (for the Lion of Judah), soldiers, strung around the room. Mobiles of these Hanukkah symbols.

CENTERPIECE

Huge "dreidel" filled with fruits, or flowers, candies or small gifts.

Miniature gifts wrapped in Hanukkah paper, or in blue and white, with chocolate or real Hanukkah "gelt" taped on top.

Large mound of chocolate Hanukkah "gelt."

REFRESHMENTS
(Recipes for dishes marked with an asterisk are given in Chapter 17.)

Grape Juice
Latkes * and Applesauce
Small Cheese Pastries and Cookies
Coffee, Milk

Purim—Feast of Esther

"And made it a day of feasting and of gladness" (Esther 8.16)

IF EVER A HOLIDAY was designed for and around a woman, Purim is it. A woman, Esther, is the heroine; the story is a romantic one. It is a story of loyalty, faith and courage. In it we are assured that despite oppression and anti-Semitism, in whatever guise, the prevailing tyrant will be overthrown ultimately.

THE STORY

THE STORY IS A MELODRAMA; it is not primarily religious. There is no reference to God in Megillat Esther (Scroll of Esther, one of the Books of the Bible). It does mention prayer and fasting, however, which has led the rabbis to explain that the religious implication was there all the time.

It is a dramatic and amazing tale, modern in every aspect. It is actually a thriller. It has a Cinderella theme—there is poor Esther who marries a king; a regicide—the killing of Vashti; a beauty contest; a suspense plot, espionage, conspirators who are apprehended, a villain who is foiled by his own evil design.

The story itself reads quickly and easily; open your Bible and see. The following is only a brief synopsis.

In the city of Shushan, King Ahasuerus of Persia is advised to search the country for a new queen since Vashti, his wife, has refused to obey his order to appear before his guests. She is removed from the throne. Simple, modest young Esther, cousin of Mordecai the Jew, wins from among hundreds of applicants the honor of being the King's consort.

The Prime Minister, scheming, arrogant Haman, sets out to punish Mordecai for refusing to bow down before him. Accordingly, he decides to exterminate all the Jews. Haman persuades the King to issue an edict ordering the destruction of all the Jews in the land. It is to be effective on the fourteenth day of Adar.

Mordecai tells Esther the sad news, pleading with her to intercede on behalf of her people. Esther appears before the King at the risk of her own life, since she has not been summoned by him. She asks him to bring Haman to a banquet she is preparing. There she discloses the fact that gallows are being set up for her cousin and reveals her own Jewish identity. The King is outraged at his Prime Minister. He issues a decree for Haman to be the victim of his own infamous plot. The fourteenth of Adar, from a day of sadness, thereby became a day of happiness and festivity.

FAST OF ESTHER   Pious Jews fast on the day before Purim in honor of Esther, who abstained from food for three days before petitioning the King.

"FEASTING AND GLADNESS"

FEASTING AND GAIETY, cookies, gifts and goodies, are prescribed right in the text of the megillah. Parties and masquerades are the order of the day. Business goes on as usual, and children attend secular school, although they usually have a holiday from Hebrew classes.

MEGILLAH READING

THE READING of the megillah in the synagogue (Purim eve) is a gay occasion. Women and children usually attend. It is the one time, in addition to Simhat Torah, when levity, even noisemaking, is permitted in the synagogue. The children are encouraged to use their "groggers" (noisemakers) each time Haman's name is mentioned. Sisterhoods frequently provide sweets for the children after the services, as "Shalach Monos" (gifts). The megillah is read again at the regular morning service on the next day.

THE SE'UDAH (MEAL OR BANQUET)

THE *se'udah* is a family get-together. You are not required to light candles, as on Shabbat or other holidays, but the meal should be "yomtovdik," festive, with special Purim dishes. The *se'udah* begins with the *motzi;* the family joins in Purim songs. The meal ends with grace in which *al hanissim* is said and the story of Purim is told.

The children might have their own celebration some time during the day (see next page), perhaps a costume party, a carnival with games and songs, or simply a jolly supper.

PURIM POINTERS

The name of this holiday, Purim (lots), is derived from the fact that Haman cast lots to discover the day most favorable for his plan for destroying the Jews.

The day after Purim is called Shushan Purim to commemorate the Jews of that city, who had to defend themselves for two days.

If children are too young to hear the megillah read directly from the Bible, read it from a children's storybook in an abbreviated version.

Purim is associated with masquerades, mumming, strolling players and pageants.

adloyada is the term used to indicate the gay quality of this holiday, the one time in the year when a Jew can get so "high" that he literally "does not know" (*adloyada*) the difference between "cursed Haman" and "blessed Mordecai."

"Hamantashen," triangle-shaped cakes, usually filled with poppy seeds (mohn) or mashed prunes, are reminders of Haman's three-cornered hat or pocket. "Kreplach" (dough filled with cheese or meat) similarly shaped, are also a Purim delicacy.

Esther's Hebrew name was Hadassah. The Women's National Zionist Organization of America, Hadassah, which came into existence on Purim, was named for her.

Purim never falls on the Sabbath.

Many anniversaries of reprieve and of deliverance have been celebrated by individual communities and families and given special Purim names.

❦ GIFTS OF THE SEASON
Megillat Esther, Queen Esther dolls, records of Purim songs.

DO plan to attend the megillah reading in the synagogue with the family.

Have a *se'udah*, a party of some kind.

Arrange a party for the children.

Have children assist in the baking of the "hamantashen" and other Purim delicacies.

Provide or make home decorations amusing and distinctive.

Provide for "Shalach Monos" (gifts); these can be simple, even cookies or cake will do.

Let the children deliver the gifts to relatives and friends.

Remember people in need and organizations, too.

See that the children have a "grogger." Some Hebrew schools provide these; if not, rattles and other noisemakers can be found in the local five-and-ten.

DON'T. Purim is one holiday when there are no "don'ts."

❦ CHILDREN'S PARTY
The preparation for a Purim party will be as much fun as the party itself. Let the children make their own masks, decorations and costumes. Centers and Hebrew schools often have Purim parties and carnivals sometime near Purim. Encourage the children to attend these.

INVITATIONS

These can be cutouts in various forms suggesting the holiday, such as megillot, *"hamantashen," or masks. Or they can be small notes or cards decorated with holiday designs. The invitation might be written by you and the children in amusing verse.*

CENTERPIECE

Characters or a scene from the megillah represented by dolls, or cardboard or paper figures.

A doll crowned and dressed as Queen Esther.

A large paper cardboard "hamentash" filled with sweets, or with "Shalach Monos," little favors for each child.

PLACECARDS

Tiny scrolls or megillot made from paper rolled on matchsticks or toothpicks.

Individual "groggers."

THE FUN

All kinds of games and quizzes are in order. A variation of "Pin the tail on the Donkey" might be "Pin the Tail on Mordecai's Horse."

🌿 PURIM SE'UDAH MENU

Recipes for dishes marked with an asterisk will be found in Chapter 17.

Grapefruit

Barley and Mushroom Soup

Roast Duck with Orange Slices

Sweet Potato Casserole

Broccoli　　　　　Salad

Hamantashen *

Tea

YOU MIGHT CHECK

The books listed on page 120 at the end of the chapter on Holy Days and Festivals all include the other holidays as well.

Some of the holidays have special books of interest:

🌿 FOR PURIM

THE PURIM ANTHOLOGY by Philip Goodman (Jewish Publication Society). Includes essays, stories, poetry, music and program material.

🌿 FOR ḤANUKKAH

THE ḤANUKKAH ANTHOLOGY by Philip Goodman (Jewish Publication Society).

ḤANUKKAH, THE FEAST OF LIGHTS by Emily Solis-Cohen, Jr. (Jewish Publication Society). Includes essays, stories, poetry, plays and program material.

CHAPTER 10

Minor Fasts and Feasts

"To everything there is a season. . . ." (Ecclesiastes 3:1)

— 10 —

Minor Fasts and Feasts

Y OUR *lu'aḥ* will remind you of some occasions that may not be too familiar to you—the minor feasts and fasts. Here is a brief discussion of these events.

TISHAH B'AV

DURING THE SUMMER, when most families are in the midst of vacations, a very significant day is observed—Tishah B'Av (the ninth of Av). This is the saddest day in the Jewish calendar.

On this date, both the first and second Temples in Jerusalem were destroyed, the first by the Babylonians in 586 B.C.E. and the second by the Romans in 70 C.E. These national disasters have never been forgotten by the Jewish people.

Other calamities in later times are said to have taken place on that day, including the expulsion of the Jews from Spain in 1492, and the Arab riots in Palestine in 1929. Despite the re-establishment of the State of Israel, in some parts of the world Jews still are persecuted. Unfortunately, Tishah B'Av continues to be a Jewish memorial day. It is a constant reminder of the long martyrdom of our ancestors, of their loyalty to the ideals and ethical principles of the Jewish religion.

THE NINE DAYS The nine days immediately preceding Tishah B'Av are generally marked by a subdued atmosphere. No weddings or public functions of a joyous nature are held. According to very strict observance, no meat or wine is served, and no new clothes are worn during this period, except on the Sabbath.

THE THREE WEEKS This annual period of mourning actually begins three weeks before Tishah B'Av, because that is when the first breach in the walls of the Temple was made. This period from the seventeenth of Tammuz to the ninth of Av is familiarly known as "the three weeks."

AT HOME Tishah B'Av is considered a day of mourning. Work goes on as usual, although it is a fast day. Since many people are away from home at this time of year, some hotels and camps have solemn services and impressive ceremonies to mark the day. Readings about the Warsaw ghetto and the war of liberation in Israel, as well as many hopeful passages, conclude the day.

IN THE SYNAGOGUE Special services are held evenings and morning, in which *kinot* (dirges) are read and *eihah* (the Book of Lamentations) are chanted.

The curtainless ark, the black drapings on the *bimah*, the candles in the dimly lit room, the worshippers sitting on low benches, convey the atmosphere of mourning.

The Sabbath preceding Tishah B'Av is called Shabbat Hazon because the first chapter of Isaiah read on that day begins with the word *hazon* (vision). The Sabbath following Tishah B'Av takes its name, Shabbat Nahamu (Sabbath of Consolation), from the opening words of the Scripture lesson:

> *Nahamu, nahamu*
> Comfort ye, comfort ye, my people,
> Saith your God,
> Bid Jerusalem take heart,
> And proclaim unto her,
> That her time of service is accomplished.
>
> (Isaiah 40:1, 2)

Throughout the Tishah B'Av literature Zion is compared to a woman. It is the "daughter of Zion" who is forsaken and the "Mother Zion" who mourns for her children.

Today mothers and daughters in this country are engaged, through various channels, in restoring the dignity of the Jewish people and rebuilding the land of Israel. This identification with the daughter of Zion motivated Hadassah (Women's National Zionist Organization of America) in making medical and health service one of its major projects. In fact, its motto was inspired by Jeremiah, who championed "the healing of the daughter of my people."

TISHAH B'AV THOUGHTS

Until 1948, Jews in Palestine prayed at the Wailing Wall. Since June 1967, united Jerusalem has afforded an opportunity for daily and holiday worship at the Western Wall. Pilgrimages are also made to David's tomb on Mount Zion.

The custom of breaking a glass under the *huppah* at the wedding ceremony is a reminder of the *hurban* (destruction), of the Temple.

When Jews pray they face east *(mizrah)* toward Jerusalem where the Temple stood.

After morning services, some people visit the cemetery.

DO circle the ninth of Av on your calendar so that you will observe the day in some way, wherever you are.

Read the Bible or relevant literature on that day.

Acquaint yourself with a synagogue in your area that has special Tishah B'Av services.

If you are in New York City on the ninth of Av, you might attend the particularly moving services at Shearith Israel (West 70th Street and Central Park West), the oldest congregation in the United States.

OTHER MINOR FASTS

Other minor fasts are:

❧ ASARAH BETEVET

Tenth of Tevet commemorates the beginning of the siege of Jerusalem which led eventually to the destruction of the first Temple.

❧ SHIVE'AH ASAR BETAMMUZ

Seventeenth of Tammuz marks the first breach made in the walls of Jerusalem by Nebuchadnezzar. This day begins "the three weeks.'

☙ TZOM GEDALIAH

The Fast of Gedaliah, which occurs on the third day of Tishri, commemorates the assassination of Gedaliah. He was a governor of Judea and a disciple of Jeremiah.

TU BISHEVAT

OUR CHILDREN are familiar with holidays for trees. In their public schools, they learn about Arbor Day; in their Hebrew schools, they learn about Tu Bishevat (fifteenth of Shevat). This holiday, sometimes called Hamishah Asar Bishevat, is also known as the New Year of the Trees.

Although Tu Bishevat comes during our winter season, in Israel the whole countryside is bursting with spring blossoms at this time. In the United States, the interest in the outdoors is highlighted at this season by the purchase of Jewish National Fund certificates for reforestation in Israel, and by the actual tasting of fruits that are grown in *eretz yisrael* (land of Israel).

Israel still observes an ancient custom, beautiful and practical. On this holiday, a tree is planted for each child born during the year—a cedar sapling for a boy, a cypress for a girl. When the child grows up and marries, branches of his tree are used for the *ḥuppah*. Trees, in our tradition, are associated with birth and marriage.

Our Torah is called *etz ḥayyim*, a tree of life.

TU BISHEVAT THOUGHTS

Provide dates, nuts, oranges, or pomegranates and bokser (carob fruit), if available, or other Israeli products.

Remember to recite the *sheheheyanu* (p. 243) when eating the new fruit.

Plan a table decoration for the family meal—the fruits mentioned above, or a group of Israeli figurines would be appropriate.

Buy a J.N.F. tree certificate, or make a donation for the J.N.F. purchase of land in Israel.

LAG BA'OMER

LAG BA'OMER, like Tu Bishevat, gets its name from a numerical abbreviation—*lag* from the letters *lamed, gimel* signifying thirty-three, plus the word *omer* (measure of grain). The counting of the *omer* starts on the second day of Pesach and continues for seven weeks, until Shavuot. These days are called the *sefirah* (counted) days.

In ancient times, during this period, it was customary to bring an *omer* of barley or wheat as an offering of thanksgiving.

During the Roman siege of Palestine in the second century C.E., a dreadful plague ravaged the countryside during the *omer* period. Tens of thousands of the pupils of Rabbi Akiba were among those who died. On the thirty-third day, the plague suddenly stopped. The *sefirah* days came to be regarded as a period of semimourning. No weddings or public celebrations are permitted in these seven weeks. On Lag Ba'omer, however, as on a few other exceptional days, the restrictions are lifted and festivity encouraged.

Lag Ba'omer recalls the last attempt of our ancestors (until 1948) to regain independence as a nation.

LAG BA'OMER LORE

BAR KOCHBA (son of the star) is one of the great heroes of this holiday. He led the rebellion against the Romans and secured the aid of the revered and saintly Rabbi Akiba.

RABBI AKIBA inspired those around him to live according to Jewish law, no matter what tortures they endured. When he was forty years old, it is said, his beautiful and loving wife Rachel urged him to give up his simple life as a shepherd to become a student of the Law. He studied, beginning with the *alef bet*, until he became the greatest scholar of his age.

SIMEON BAR YOCHAI hid in a cave for many years in order to be able to continue his teaching, despite Roman decrees forbidding the study of the Torah. The students who came to see him disguised themselves as hunters, carrying bows and arrows. It is said that Bar Yochai died on Lag Ba'Omer, and that in his last request, he asked that his "yahrzeit" be observed by celebration rather than mourning.

ISRAELIS celebrate the day with great joy. Hundreds of pious Hassidim come from all parts of the land to Meron, a village near Safed, where Bar Yochai lived, to honor the great teacher and the ideals for which he stood. They chant psalms, sing Hassidic songs, and study the Zohar (the holy book ascribed to Bar Yochai).

IN AMERICA, we hold campfire gatherings, reminiscent of bonfires in Israel, around which stories are told and horas danced. Children go on outings, picnics and field days. As they play with bow and arrow and take part in archery contests, they recall the brave scholars disguised as hunters. Pageants and plays depicting the Lag Ba'omer stories are highlighted in Hebrew schools and clubs.

LAG BA'OMER is also known as Scholars' Day.

There is no reference in the prayer book to Lag Ba'omer.

There are no special blessings for the occasion.

🌿 GIFTS OF THE SEASON

For the children, archery sets, modern Israeli coins or facsimiles of historic ones.

YOM HA'ATZMAUT

THE ESTABLISHMENT of the State of Israel on the fifth of Iyar, in 1948 (that year it was May 14), has given us a new celebration—

Yom Ha'atzmaut (Israel Independence Day). Though this day has not yet acquired traditional character, it is an occasion for great rejoicing.

In Israel, there are mass parades with floats and pageantry, special concerts and performances, home parties and dancing in the streets.

In America, pageants, public meetings and special programs, featured by various organizations, mark the occasion.

YOM HASHO'AH — DAY OF THE HOLOCAUST

ON APRIL 12, 1951 the Knesset enacted a resolution declaring the 27th day of Nisan as Yom Hasho'ah, a remembrance day for the Holocaust and the revolt of the ghettos. Since that time, it has been observed, to varying degrees, throughout this continent.

YOM HAZIKARON — DAY OF MEMORIAL

AFTER THE spectacularly victorious Six-Day War of June, 1967, Jerusalem was reunited. Many ancient historic and religious shrines and sites, previously inaccessible to citizens of Israel, were opened to visitors and tourists of all religions.

But the price for the "liberation" was heavy, and a Day of Memorial—Yom Hazikaron—to those who died in Zion's cause is observed annually on the eve of Independence Day.

CHAPTER 11

American Holidays

"America! America! God shed His grace on thee,
And crown Thy good with brotherhood from sea to shining
sea"

(America the Beautiful)

11

American Holidays

THE FAMILY CELEBRATES many different occasions during the year—birthdays, graduations, Bar Mitzvahs, engagements, weddings and anniversaries. Nations, too, celebrate birthdays and anniversaries. Our country has Columbus Day, Armistice or Veterans' Day, Memorial or Decoration Day, Labor Day, Lincoln's and Washington's birthdays, Election Day, Independence Day (July 4th) and Thanksgiving Day.

Not all these days receive the same emphasis or enthusiasm throughout the United States, but Thanksgiving Day is the one day that all the American people have taken to their hearts.

THANKSGIVING DAY

THANKSGIVING is a home-centered holiday. All the magazines, the radio and television emphasize the homecoming of the children and grandchildren, the aromatic atmosphere in the house, the jollity and wholesomeness of the gathering. The spirit of thankfulness is in the air.

This holiday draws its inspiration from the Bible; our founding fathers celebrated their Thanksgiving in a religious mood. Today, in many communities, synagogues and temples join with churches in Thanksgiving services. The proclamation by the President of the United States is usually printed in the newspapers and broadcast across the country.

PATRIOTIC HOLIDAYS

THE AMERICAN JEWISH WOMAN should do what she can to give greater depth and meaning to the other great milestones in our nation's history. For example, she should try to recapture the spirit that motivated George Washington to set aside the Fourth of July as a day of prayer.

This holiday lends itself well to festive motifs in table settings, food and decorations. Every newspaper and woman's magazine offers helpful suggestions at this time. It is not only appropriate but important that we make our American holidays significant and beautiful for our families.

TAKE NOTE   Halloween and St. Valentine's Day, however, despite their tremendous popularity, are not national holidays. They started as saints' days. (Halloween was formerly known as All Hallows or All Saints, and the reference in St. Valentine's Day is obvious.) Although the nature of their celebration today has come far from their religious origin, they are still inappropriate for Jewish home participation.

CHRISTMAS AND EASTER   Christmas and Easter require special comment. These are the holiest days in the Christian calendar, in spite of the secularization by some through radio, TV and commercial enterprises.

Jews should recognize and respect the religious quality of their friends' and neighbors' holidays. Although they may respond to the season's greetings of their non-Jewish friends and associates, it is quite out of place for Jews to introduce the spirit of Christmas or Easter into their own homes. The use of Christmas or Easter symbols, even secularized ones like the Christmas tree or lights, or the Easter eggs or bunny, are absolutely out of place in a Jewish home.

However, just as your children might want to invite their non-Jewish friends to a Hanukkah or Purim party, they may want to accept invitations to their Christian friends' homes at Christmastime or Easter.

Parents of school children may be troubled by Christmas and Easter activity in the school. The principle of separation of church and state is implicit in our constitution. Unfortunately, this does not prevent the celebration of Christmas and Easter in public schools throughout the land. There are Jews who think they are serving the Jewish cause by asking for "equal time" for Hanukkah celebrations in the school. This is wrong for two reasons: first, all religious holidays should be kept out of schools, and second, Hanukkah should not be made a pale imitation of Christmas. It is certainly undesirable for Jewish boys and girls to participate in nativity plays and similar religious celebrations. Where there is a local problem, do not take any individual action, consult your rabbi, who will probably get in touch with the National Jewish Community Relations Advisory Council.

NEW YEAR'S EVE New Year's Eve is gaily celebrated as the beginning of a new secular year. Since this is a high point in the social calendar year, check the day of the week on which it falls. If you find that a Jewish group to which you or your husband belong is planning a New Year's Eve party on Friday evening, suggest a change of date to them. Certainly you will recognize that New Year's Eve hilarity is not in keeping with the Sabbath.

The Jewish religious holidays do not commemorate people or founders. Most of them are reminders of great ideas and ideals, such as freedom on Pesach; thanksgiving to God on Sukkot; ethical principles on Shavuot; universality of man on Rosh Hashanah and Yom Kippur. All the holidays stress peace. Together with the American holidays, these give us a very rich calendar.

❧ THANKSGIVING DINNER

Fruit Cup
Consommé
Turkey with Chestnut Dressing
Cranberry Sauce
Sweet Potato or Squash Casserole
Tossed Salad
Apple or Pumpkin Pie
Nuts Candies
Black Coffee Tea

❧ FOURTH OF JULY

Tomato Juice with Sour Cream
Fresh Salmon with Sauce
Small Potatoes with Parsley   Peas
Sliced Tomatoes
Fourth of July Cake
(Cake with white icing decorated with little flags or with red
maraschino cherries and blue icing trim.)
Iced Coffee

DO plan a One World Party during United Nations Week if you live in a community with people of varied national backgrounds.

Read the Declaration of Independence on the Fourth of July.

Feature an appropriate decorative theme for your table, if you are entertaining on or near an American holiday.

YOU AND YOUR CHILDREN WILL FIND MATERIAL ON OUR AMERICAN HOLIDAYS IN THE SCHOOL AND PUBLIC LIBRARY

❧ BOOKS ABOUT AMERICAN JEWISH HEROES

WHAT THE LIBERTY BELL PROCLAIMED by Leon Spitz (Women's League). Gives stories of the part Jews played in American history during the Colonial period and through the Civil War. The children might enjoy reading this around the Fourth of July or Lincoln's or Washington's birthdays.

JEWISH ADVENTURES IN AMERICA by Elma Ehrlich Levinger (Bloch Publishing Company). Highlights Jewish history through biographies of Jewish men and women.

GIANTS ON THE EARTH by Deborah Pessin (Behrman House). Includes stories of Jewish heroes in American history.

Of course, biographies of great Americans, stories of the pioneers, history and historical novels make good holiday reading.

CHAPTER 12

A Goodly Heritage

"How beautiful is our heritage!" (Siddur)

—— 12 ——

A Goodly Heritage

MOST COMMUNITIES have at least one temple or synagogue. Your family background, your traditional beliefs will determine whether you join a Conservative, Orthodox or Reform temple. Certainly the physical appearance of the structure, the dominant social set, the convenience of a nearby Hebrew school car pool should not be factors determining your choice.

THE SYNAGOGUE

TODAY, IN THE LARGE CITY, in the small town, as well as in the suburbs, the house of worship again becomes the focus of Jewish life. The synagogue, Hebrew school and community center are frequently under one roof. Many important ceremonies, from the naming of a child to the wedding, take place in the synagogue.

The synagogue or temple is called by many names:

> *bet hatefillah*—House of Prayer
> *bet hakenesset*—House of Assembly
> *bet hamidrash*—House of Study

IN THE SYNAGOGUE Though the design and architecture of the synagogue may vary from traditional to ultramodern, the following must be present:

THE TORAH (SCROLL OF THE LAW). The Torah is a hand-written parchment scroll of the first five books of the Bible, known as the Five Books of Moses, the Pentateuch, or the *humash*. It is the most sacred object in the synagogue. There are often several scrolls in the Ark. It is an old tradition to adorn the scrolls. They may be covered with velvet or other fine fabrics, topped with silver crowns or bells of artistic workmanship, and enhanced by decorative breastplates. The *yad* is a silver pointer used by the reader of the Torah.

THE ARON HAKODESH (HOLY ARK). The Ark is the cabinet which contains the Torah scrolls. It is so situated in the synagogue that congregants turn east to face it in prayer. The congregation customarily rises whenever the Ark is open and remains standing until the Ark is closed.

THE PAROHET (CURTAIN). A curtain or drapery hangs in front of the Ark to separate the "holy of holies" from the rest of the synagogue. Most of the year it may be a blue, purple or scarlet curtain. During the High Holy Days, a white curtain is sometimes used. On Tishah B'Av, the curtain is removed entirely, as a sign of mourning.

NER TAMID (ETERNAL LIGHT). The perpetual light suspended over the Ark, symbolizing the undying faith of Israel.

THE MENORAH (CANDELABRUM). A symbolic reminder of the seven branched candelabrum that was in the original Temple. It also signifies the light that is the Torah.

THE BIMAH (PLATFORM). The pulpit or platform from which the Torah is read.

THE AMUD (READING STAND). The lectern at which the cantor or reader stands to lead the congregation in prayer.

SYNAGOGUE OFFICIALS
rabbi—spiritual leader of the congregation
hazzan—cantor responsible for the musical portion of the service
ba'al tefillah—reader of the service
ba'al tekiah—blower of the shofar
shamash—sexton in charge of ritual paraphernalia

THE SERVICE   The synagogue service follows a definite pattern, recognizing the need for communal prayer.

Services are held daily:
In the morning (*shaharit*),

In the afternoon (*minhah*), and
In the evening (*ma'ariv*).
On holidays there is an additional service—*musaf*.
Yom Kippur has a special closing service—*ne'ilah*.
THE SIDDUR (PRAYER BOOK). Contains the prayers for weekdays
and Sabbath services, with additional portions for holiday services,
as well as the grace, blessings and psalms for various occasions.
THE MAHZOR. This is a special festival prayer book.
NOTE: It is best to provide yourself with the particular Siddur
and Mahzor used by your synagogue.

TORAH READING A section of the Torah is read on the Sabbath,
new moons, festivals and semi-holidays, and on Monday and
Thursday mornings. The Torah is divided into fifty-four sections,
called *parashot* or *sidrot*. One *parashah* or *sidrah* is read each
week so that the reading of the Torah is completed within the
year. On Simhat Torah, the final verses of Deuteronomy are read,
and the annual cycle immediately begins again with verses from
Genesis.

On Sabbaths and festivals, the Torah portion is followed by the
reading of a specific section of the Prophets, usually having some
relationship to the companion *sidrah*. This selection is called
Haftarah.

THE BOOK OF BOOKS

THE BIBLE (from the Greek and Latin word "biblia" meaning
book) is frequently referred to as the Holy Scriptures. The Jewish
people never speak of the Bible as the Old Testament. The Hebrew word *tanah* also denotes the Bible; each of its syllables actually describes one of the three sections:

> *ta*—Torah (Five Books of Moses)
> *na*—*nevi'im* (Prophets)
> *h*—*ketuvim* (Writings)

Torah—called *humash*, from the Hebrew word for five. The
Greek word "Pentateuch" (five books) is also used for this section.
    nevi'im—divides into two parts, Early Prophets and Later
Prophets.
    ketuvim—also referred to as the "Hagiographa" (Greek for holy
writings).

The chart (opposite page) outlines the books of the Bible.

An acquaintance with the Bible is considered part of any educated woman's background; certainly it is a necessary part of her Jewish education. When you attend services regularly you will read the First Five Books as well as some parts of the Prophets.

You might also read selections from the Holy Scriptures in English at home. The Jewish Publication Society translation is highly recommended. *Pathways Through the Bible* by Mortimer J. Cohen (Jewish Publication Society), is a simplified condensed presentation of the Bible. The *Pentateuch and Haftorahs* by Dr. J. H. Hertz, with Hebrew text, English translation and commentary, is a good addition to the family library.

You might like to join a Bible study course conducted by your rabbi, adult education institute, Sisterhood or other group.

APOCRYPHA Certain books were for one reason or another not included in the official canon or collection of inspired writings, the Bible. These are called the "Apocrypha," which means hidden. They include, among others, the Books of the Maccabees, Judith, Tobit, Ecclesiasticus or The Wisdom of Ben Sira.

BASIC BOOKS

IN ADDITION TO THE BIBLE, certain books have been a part of the fabric of Judaism for centuries. A lifetime of study could be devoted to each of them. The outline here is merely a glossary:

❧ TALMUD. Collection of writings, including law and legend, interpretations of Scripture and ethical precepts. After the Bible, this is the most important spiritual document of the Jewish people. It is divided into two main parts:

MISHNAH. (Statement of the Law.) A compilation of oral discussions and interpretations relating to the Bible, completed by the end of the second century C.E.

GEMARAH. Discussions and commentaries relating to the Mishnah. Completed at about the end of the fifth century C.E.

❧ MIDRASH. *Midrashim,* or sermonic interpretations of Biblical literature preserved through the centuries, are explanations of the Scriptures through homilies, designed to popularize them among the masses of Jews. (Please turn to page 160.)

BOOKS OF THE BIBLE

TORAH — THE LAW
(Five Books of Moses)

Genesis (bereshit)
Exodus (shemot)
Leviticus (vayikra)
Numbers (bemidbar)
Deuteronomy (devarim)

NEVI'IM — THE PROPHETS

Joshua	Jeremiah	Micah
Judges	Ezekiel	Nahum
Samuel I	Hosea	Habakkuk
Samuel II	Joel	Zephaniah
Kings I	Amos	Haggai
Kings II	Obadiah	Zechariah
Isaiah	Jonah	Malachi

KETUVIM — THE WRITINGS

Psalms	Esther
Proverbs	Daniel
Job	Ezra
Song of Songs	Nehemiah
Ruth	Chronicles I
Lamentations	Chronicles II
Ecclesiastes	

❧ SHULCHAN ARUCH. A code of laws presented in simple form. The literal meaning of the phrase *shulḥan aruḥ* is a "set table." The work was created in the sixteenth century and deals with ritual and legal questions in Jewish life.

❧ RASHI. These letters are used to represent the name and the works of the most distinguished commentator on the Bible and the Talmud, a rabbi who lived in the eleventh century C.E.

❧ PIRKE AVOT (Perek). Ethics of the Fathers. A unique collection, in the Mishnah, of the favorite sayings of the Jewish sages. You can find it in the Siddur.

The average Jewish woman may not be as familiar as her husband is with the names and significance of many of the objects in the synagogue, or with the basic books of the Jewish heritage. This chapter attempts to give you only a "vocabulary"—terms of reference. The best place to learn about the synagogue is in the house of worship; the place to learn about the books is in a study course.

"Whoso honors the Torah, he himself will be honored" (Pirke Avot).

FOR YOUR PERMANENT HOME LIBRARY

❧ YOU WILL SURELY WANT TO INCLUDE

THE HOLY SCRIPTURES. The Jewish Publication Society edition, either in English translation or in an edition with parallel columns in Hebrew and English.

HERTZ CHUMASH by Joseph H. Hertz (Soncino). The Pentateuch and Haftorahs with commentary by Hertz. Hebrew-English.

❧ YOU MIGHT ALSO LIKE TO ADD THESE

HAMMER ON THE ROCK: A MIDRASH READER edited by Nahum N. Glatzer (Schocken, hardcover and paperback). Two hundred representative passages from the Talmud and Midrash.

PIRKE AVOT, or Sayings of the Fathers. There are many available editions, such as the translation by Rabbi Joseph H. Hertz with accompanying Hebrew text and commentary, published by Behrman House.

THE ETHICS OF THE TALMUD: SAYINGS OF THE FATHERS translation and commentary by R. Travers Herford (Schocken, hardcover and paperback). Comprehensive guide for the English reader. Text is printed in both Hebrew and English.

THE LIVING TALMUD, selected and translated with an essay by Judah Goldin (New American Library; paper).

🌱 ON THE BIBLE AND OTHER GREAT BOOKS

PATHWAYS THROUGH THE BIBLE by Mortimer J. Cohen, with illustrations by Arthur Szyk (Jewish Publication Society). The text of the Scriptures rearranged for easy reading, with an introductory comment for each book of the Bible.

LEGENDS OF THE BIBLE by Louis Ginzberg (Simon and Schuster). An abbreviated one-volume edition of this scholar's *Legends of the Jews.*

CERTAIN PEOPLE OF THE BOOK by Maurice Samuel (Alfred A. Knopf). Personalities of the Scriptures with Samuel's brilliant interpretation and comment.

EVERYMAN'S TALMUD by Dr. A. Cohen (E. P. Dutton and Company). A comprehensive summary of the Talmud and its teachings on ethics, religion, folklore and law.

THE BIBLE: A MODERN JEWISH APPROACH by Bernard J. Bamberger (Schocken Paperback). A concise introduction to the Hebrew Scriptures, their literary structure and the chief concepts of God, man, and society.

THE GREAT JEWISH BOOKS and their influence on history, edited by Samuel Caplan and Harold Ribalow (Horizon Press). The twelve most important books (including the Bible, Talmud, Rashi, etc.) discussed, with selections from each.

THE WORLD OF THE TALMUD by Morris Adler (Schocken Paperback). A guide to the Talmud and its historic background, and an introduction to the life and thought of the Talmudic sages.

🌱 ON THE PRAYER BOOK AND THE SYNAGOGUE SERVICE

SERVICE OF THE HEART by Dr. Evelyn Garfiel (National Academy for Advanced Jewish Studies of the United Synagogue of America). A well-written, lucid guide to an understanding of the prayer book. It includes a description of the history and function of the Siddur, the significance of the various prayers, and an explanation of home and synagogue services.

MY BOOK OF PRAYER: SABBATH AND WEEKDAYS

MY BOOK OF PRAYER: HOLIDAYS AND HOLY DAYS by Rabbi Hyman Chanover and Evelyn Zusman, illustrated by Leonard Weisgard (United Synagogue Commission on Jewish Education). Prayers in English and Hebrew for every home occasion, with handsome illustrations. Excellent gift book for young children.

JUSTICE AND MERCY by Max Arzt (Holt, Reinhart and Winston, hardcover and paperback). Sound popular interpretations of High Holy Day prayers.

THE HIGH HOLY DAYS by Herman Kieval (Burning Bush Press). Commentary on the Prayer Book for Rosh Hashanah and Yom Kippur.

A TIME TO PRAY by Rose Goldstein (Women's League). Commentary on and discussion of the daily prayer book.

CHAPTER 13

The Fine Art of Learning

"He who does not increase his knowledge, decreases it"
(Pirke Avot)

—— 13 ——

The Fine Art of Learning

IT IS POSSIBLE for every child to receive a good Jewish education today. The important thing is that you enroll your child,
boy or girl, for this education in his early years; that you encourage respect for learning, and see that study is continued, if at
all possible, well beyond the elementary school level. This is as
true for the girl as it is for the boy. In her future role as wife and
mother, the girl will be a forceful influence in the home.

A COMPLETE HEBREW EDUCATION

HEBREW EDUCATION is available from the foundation school level
through institutions of higher learning. You and your husband
will probably consider the merits of the different kinds of schools
and discuss them with your rabbi.

THE DAY SCHOOL   If you want your children to have the maximum in Jewish education, the day school is the happy answer.
There is a steady increase in modern, well-staffed, attractively and
efficiently appointed day schools which combine Jewish studies
and the regular elementary school curriculum. A few of these
schools continue through the four year high school course. The
children become equally at home in Hebrew and in English sub-

jects. The day schools more than adequately meet the requirements of the public school system. They have a complete program
of extracurricular activities.

THE WEEKDAY AFTERNOON SCHOOL If you want your children
to study after public school hours, the congregational weekday
afternoon school with three to five sessions a week, gives a satisfactory course of study on Jewish history, the Bible, customs and
ceremonies, current events, and a reading familiarity with the
prayer book in Hebrew.

There are also congregational schools which have classes one
day a week, most frequently on Sundays. There is an increasing
recognition that this course of Jewish study is very limited.

In some cities, the religious groups jointly organize a Talmud
Torah, a non-synagogue weekday Hebrew school which meets
several afternoons a week.

Bar Mitzvah and Bat Mitzvah are high points in the child's education but not stopping places. Many boys and girls continue their
Hebrew studies in the Hebrew high school, where they are given
a more concentrated course of study which includes the Bible,
Talmud and commentaries, medieval and modern Hebrew literature, Jewish philosophy, religion and history, Jewish music, and
modern Israel.

THE NURSERY SCHOOL You might be interested to know that
many congregations and community centers sponsor a foundation
or nursery school for the pre-school child, with a regular nursery
school program plus Jewish orientation through play, art, songs
and dramatization.

HIGHER EDUCATION If your child wants a more advanced Jewish
education, perhaps leading to teaching or social work in the Jewish field, or a rabbinical degree, there are good schools under
Conservative, Orthodox, and Reform auspices.

The Jewish Theological Seminary in New York City (Conservative) includes a rabbinical and a cantorial school, a teachers' institute, Seminary College of Jewish Studies, Women's League Institute. The West Coast branch of the Seminary is located in Los
Angeles, California.

Yitzhak Elchanan Yeshiva in New York City and Hebrew Theological College in Chicago, Illinois as well as other rabbinical

colleges train rabbis, teachers and religious functionaries for Orthodox congregations.

Hebrew Union College—Institute of Religion in Cincinnati, Ohio, with branches in New York City and Los Angeles trains rabbis, cantors, teachers and social workers in the Jewish community service fields, for Reform congregations.

Other schools specializing in the preparation of teachers in the Jewish field include Herzliah Hebrew Teachers' Institute, New York City; Gratz College, Philadelphia, Pennsylvania; College of Jewish Studies, Chicago, Illinois; Hebrew Teachers College, Brookline, Massachusetts.

There are other schools of higher learning of special interest to the Jewish boy and girl. These include Yeshiva University in New York, which gives courses toward an academic degree plus courses in Jewish history, religion, Bible, and Hebrew. This university also has graduate schools in Jewish education, Jewish social service and general Jewish studies and a liberal arts woman's college, Stern College for Women. A non-sectarian medical school, Albert Einstein Medical College, in New York City, is also part of Yeshiva University.

Brandeis University in Waltham, Massachusetts, is the first Jewish sponsored non-sectarian undergraduate college in the western hemisphere.

Dropsie College for Hebrew and Cognate Learning in Philadelphia is a non-sectarian, non-theological postgraduate college. Its courses lead to degrees of Master of Arts, Doctor of Education and Doctor of Philosophy. It trains people for government, social and educational agencies in the United States and Israel.

Quite a few universities have departments of Jewish studies. The Hebrew language and Jewish history are included in the curriculum of many colleges and universities. More and more, public high schools are giving accredited courses in Hebrew as a modern language.

WHEN YOUR CHILD GOES TO COLLEGE

THE COLLEGE STUDENT finds it possible to maintain Jewish contact even when far from home. Most colleges have a Hillel Foundation (a project of B'nai B'rith), or other Jewish groups which plan cultural religious fellowship and interfaith activities on the campus. They also provide personal guidance when necessary.

Encourage your child, both before and during college, to affiliate with the national junior Jewish groups such as the youth organizations of the synagogue, ATID, Leaders Training Fellowship, United Synagogue Youth; or Zionist groups, such as Hashachar, Senior Judea; or the youth groups of service organizations, such as B'nai B'rith Youth Organization (Alep Zadek Aleph).

STUDY IN ISRAEL

THERE ARE AN INCREASING NUMBER of summer institutes, year-long study programs and special trips in Israel available for both children and adults. For most current information consult your child's Hebrew school principal, your boy's or girl's college, or the Jewish Agency, 515 Park Avenue, New York, N. Y. 10022.

The Jewish Agency arranges a summer institute for American and Canadian students and teachers and others between the ages of eighteen and thirty. An orientation period precedes a tour of Israel and a period of working at an agricultural settlement. Tours and lectures are conducted in English; Hebrew instruction is part of the daily program. The trip is made by plane; the cost is kept low. Applicants can register through organizations such as United Synagogue Youth, National Federation of Temple Youth, Young Judea, B'nai B'rith, Boy Scouts of America.

The Agency also arranges a year's study in an institute for youth leaders for boys and girls aged seventeen to twenty-two. The year is divided into seven months of study and five months of work at an agricultural settlement. College credit can be arranged for this year.

At the Hebrew University a year's study can be arranged for American college students for their sophomore or junior year. Some theological seminaries and the major Jewish teacher-training schools make it possible for their students to have a year of study in Israel.

Many organizations arrange study or study-work tours in Israel. For example: The United Synagogue has an Autumn kibbutz Ulpan for High School graduates; Young Judea offers a year in Israel for seventeen to twenty year olds; B'nai Akiba (Orthodox

Zionist organization) arranges for a study in a yeshiva and work in a settlement; Habonim (Labor Zionist Youth) arranges a labor-study program for young people.

Scholarships are available in many cases. All the tours and institutes are planned to keep the cost as moderate as possible.

WHEN SUMMER COMES

FINE CAMPS ARE AVAILABLE to the Jewish child in many parts of the United States and Canada; these provide all the normal advantages of camping plus the positive values of Jewish education and religious experience in a pleasant environment. These summer camps may be privately owned or run by community centers, educational groups and other organizations, or under the auspices of youth movements. The American Zionist Youth Commission, the YMHA-YWHA, B'nai B'rith, Habonim, all run camps—to name a few. In some Boy Scout camps, provision is made for those who observe kashrut.

The programs of the camps vary widely. Some observe the dietary laws strictly; some merely have "Jewish-type" food. Many include projects in Jewish music, drama, dance, arts and crafts. In many, religious services and holiday celebrations are a regular part of the program.

Some have classes in Hebrew study and Hebrew conversation; some are completely Hebrew-speaking.

HEBREW-SPEAKING CAMPS Two of the best known Hebrew-speaking camps in the United States are Ramah and Masad. Both are non-profit; both observe the dietary laws and both are for boys and girls. Ramah is organized by the United Synagogue of America and the Jewish Theological Seminary. Camps are located in Massachusetts, Pennsylvania, Wisconsin, California and Canada. Ramah conducts a Jewish educational program in its camps, with some formal instruction in Hebrew.

Masad is conducted by the Histadruth Ivrith of America (1841 Broadway, New York, N. Y. 10023). Two camps are located in Pennsylvania and one in Canada. The complete camp program is conducted in Hebrew.

DAY BY DAY For children who remain in town, there are day camps; these are frequently connected with a Jewish center or school. Here, in addition to the usual day camp program, the child develops Jewish values in creative activity like puppetry, drawings, dancing and singing.

CHOOSING A CAMP In deciding on a camp (day or away-from-home), consider carefully first your child's needs and interests, then what the camp has to offer. A child should *go* to camp, not *be sent*.

Meet the director.
Get to know some of the counselors.
Visit the camp, when possible.
Check the food arrangements, the health and safety programs.
Look into the age groupings.
Inquire how the children spend their day.

Information and directories on day camps and camps away from home can be obtained from:

National Jewish Welfare Board
New York

American Camping Association
New York

Association of Private Camps
New York

For holiday camps and schools abroad, see the Jewish Travel Guide described on page 198.

NOTE: The Jewish camp field offers fine opportunities for counseling jobs for boys and girls.

ADULTS CAN LEARN, TOO

WITH INCREASED LEISURE TIME and since the establishment of the State of Israel, adult Jewish studies have become an accepted part of American community life. Courses, lectures, seminars, and study groups for men and women are conducted by synagogues, centers, men's clubs, Sisterhoods, organizations like B'nai B'rith, Hadassah, National Council of Jewish Women, ORT, Mizrachi, and by seminaries and institutes.

You will find opportunities ranging from a one-day annual forum to a course that meets several hours weekly. You can find subjects from a discussion of the Sabbath to an understanding of the United Nations special agencies, from an evening's session on how to conduct a Seder to a twenty week course on modern Hebrew literature.

Of this you can be sure: Whatever your interest and need in Jewish education, whatever your background, you can find what you want easily and find it, very often, quite close to home. Ask your rabbi, check at your center, inquire from the leaders of the local Jewish women's organizations. If you live in a small community where there are no study groups, initiate one.

Watch for workshops, often given before a particular holiday at your synagogue or Jewish center, to review the history, significance and ceremonies connected with the holiday. Even if you have the basic information, you may get new insights or practical suggestions.

Your local newspaper may announce visiting lecturers, special concerts or exhibits. In New York City, there are courses, lectures and exhibits at many places, including the Jewish Theological Seminary, the Theodore Herzl Institute, the Jewish Museum, Hebrew Union College, and the Herzliah Hebrew Teachers Institute.

In addition to the formal and informal programs of adult education, congregations and organizations sometimes schedule weekend institutes and retreats in which concentrated study can be enjoyed in a relaxed (usually countryside) atmosphere.

WHY HEBREW?

No ONE ANY LONGER RATIONALIZES about the need for the study of Hebrew. Hebrew is the language of worship of the Jewish religion throughout the world. Hebrew is the key to a classic literature of the experiences and history of an ancient people. Hebrew is a link of world Jewry to the state of Israel. Hebrew is the bond of the past, present and future of creative Jewish life.

You Know More Hebrew Than You Think   The words "jubilee" and "amen" are Hebrew in origin and only two of many examples. If you speak Yiddish, you are using Hebrew a good deal of the time. Words like "rachmonus" (pity), "simchah" (joy), are part of our everyday vocabulary. Almost all of us wish each other a "good yom tov," literally, a "good day."

The central agency for the advancement of Hebrew culture is the Histadruth Ivrith of America, 1841 Broadway, New York, N. Y. 10023. It sponsors Hebrew cultural and educational activities, and organizes Hebrew study circles. It features a concentrated course in the Hebrew language called "Ulpan," and also helps support *Hadoar* magazine.

Increasing travel in Israel has been a spur to the study of the language. Many communities and organizations are arranging pilgrimages to Israel for adults, which give them the opportunity of seeing the land under expert guidance and at moderate cost. But the interest in the Hebrew goes much deeper than its current use as the secular language of a new country.

"It is the Jewish tradition and the Jewish law and the Jewish spirit which prepares for the lessons of life." (Brandeis.)

DO start your children's Jewish education early.

Join the parent-teacher organization of your child's Hebrew school as well as his public school. Attend the meetings, support its projects. Examine the books and materials used in the school.

Give the boy or girl entering college a Bible and a Prayer Book.

Remind your boy or girl, home for the holidays, to attend special youth services or social functions when these are arranged by the rabbi for college students.

Learn Hebrew with your children, just as you might follow along with their music lessons.

Investigate the series of long-playing records teaching modern conversational Hebrew (see below).

Subscribe to *Hadoar* (page 172).

Participate in the events of these special months as they occur annually:

Jewish Book Month
Jewish Education Month
Jewish Music Month
Hebrew Month

DON'T terminate your child's education with Bar Mitzvah or Bat Mitzvah.

Don't neglect your daughter's Hebrew education.

THESE MIGHT BE USEFUL

❦ ON HEBREW

HEBREW SELF-TAUGHT by Zevi and Ben-Ami Scharfstein (Zionist Organization of America with the co-operation of the Histadruth Ivrith of America). Explanation of the alphabet and its phonetics. Step-by-step lessons; informal style.

LIVING HEBREW by Dr. Samuel Steinberg (prepared in co-operation with the Seminary School of Jewish Studies of the Jewish Theological Seminary). Forty lessons in four long-playing records (recorded by native Israelis). A complete language course, beginning with the alphabet and sounds of the language. Israeli pronunciation used. With the records comes a manual containing the text of each lesson, translations and a summary of grammar. Also a common-usage dictionary.

HEBREW, THE ETERNAL LANGUAGE by William Chomsky (Jewish Publication Society). A readable and authoritative "biography" of the Hebrew language. It tells the story from the beginnings in Canaan to the most recent developments in Israel.

WHY STUDY HEBREW?—a pamphlet by Samuel M. Blumenfeld (Department of Education and Culture of the Jewish Agency) that supplies some authoritative answers.

PILGRIMAGE HEBREW (Hadassah Education Department). "A Handbook of Tourist Hebrew," an attractive pamphlet designed to help build a basic vocabulary for travel in Israel.

❧ PAMPHLETS ON EDUCATION

YOUR CHILD AND YOU by Azriel Eisenberg (United Synagogue of America, Commission on Jewish Education).

DEAR PARENT by Azriel Eisenberg (Jewish Education Committee of New York).

CHAPTER 14

Self-Service

"Who is worthy of honor? He who respects his fellow-men"
(Pirke Avot)

—— 14 ——

Self-Service

YOU AND YOUR HUSBAND will enjoy associating yourselves, as members of the Jewish community, with Jewish activities, not only in the synagogue but in other areas.

FOR THE WHOLE FAMILY

THE JEWISH CENTER gives the whole family, from the nursery toddler to its senior citizen, a chance to participate in Jewish life in an American environment.

The facilities of the center often include class or clubrooms, a library, an auditorium, a gymnasium and a swimming pool. The nursery school, Hebrew school and day camp discussed in Chapter 13 are frequently important parts of the center.

It sponsors a wide range of clubs and activities of general and Jewish interest for all age levels. These often include dramatic, choral, dance, music, photography, arts and crafts, painting, stamp and swimming groups. The center often arranges lectures, forums and adult education courses.

NOW IS THE TIME   Get acquainted with your center and become a member. In most cases, the dues are nominal in comparison to the benefits which the whole family enjoys. Make use of its library—it may have current books and magazines of Jewish interest, as well as the classics of literature.

You and your husband will find it easy to enroll for the course in Hebrew that you've been meaning to take, to enjoy that hobby you've postponed starting, or to attend a workshop explaining Jewish holiday customs. Your children will benefit from these group experiences and will gain opportunities to develop leadership as Jews and Americans. An elderly relative may find congenial companionship in a Senior Citizen or Golden Age group.

TZEDAKAH—A WAY OF LIFE

THE CENTER ALSO SERVES as the meeting place and home of many Jewish organizations. Some of these will be concerned with giving, not only philanthropy but service.

The practice of charity is a basic principle of Jewish life. The Torah explicitly commands it:

"And thou shalt not glean thy vineyard, neither shalt
thou gather the fallen fruit of thy vineyard; thou
shalt leave them for the poor and for the stranger. . . ."
(Leviticus 19:10)

Reference to the virtue of giving occurs frequently in the Talmud. The word *tzedakah* actually means "righteousness."

Maimonides, the great Jewish philosopher and physician of the twelfth century, outlined eight degrees of charity which decrease in merit in relation to the method of giving. The first—preventing poverty by teaching a person a trade or setting him up in business —is very modern in its point of view. This principle guides many of the organizations which will be described later in this chapter.

The famous last section of Proverbs, in describing "A woman of valour . . ." says:

"She stretcheth out her hand to the poor;
Yea, she reacheth forth her hands to the needy."
(Proverbs 31:10)

Organized philanthropies or institutions deal with most needy cases today. You may want to give your time to both non-sectarian and Jewish organizations.

THE COMMUNITY IN GENERAL   The non-sectarian activities will include local appeals for hospitals or community institutions,

EIGHT DEGREES OF CHARITY

There are eight degrees in the giving of charity, one higher than the other.

1. The highest degree, than which there is nothing higher, is to take hold of a person who has been crushed and to give him a gift or a loan, or to enter into partnership with him, or to find work for him, and thus put him on his feet that he will not be dependent on his fellow men. . . .

2. Lower in degree to this is the one who gives charity, *tzedakah,* to the poor, but does not know to whom he gives it, nor does the poor man know from whom he received it. . . .

3. Lower in degree to this is when the giver knows to whom he gives, but the poor does not know from whom he receives. . . .

4. Lower in degree to this is when the poor knows from whom he receives, but the giver does not know to whom he gives. . . .

5. Lower in degree to this is when one gives even before he is asked. . . .

6. Lower in degree to this is when one gives after he has been asked. . . .

7. Lower in degree to this is when one gives less than he should, but graciously. . . .

8. Lower in degree to this is when one gives grudgingly. . . .

—*Moses Maimonides*

and national drives such as those for Girl Scouts, Boy Scouts, Red Cross, Salvation Army, Heart, Cancer, Cerebral Palsy, Muscular Dystrophy, Mentally Retarded, etc.

Of course, you will make your contribution as generous as your budget allows. In addition, try to co-operate in the block drives. When your community chairman calls you, take an area to cover or give time for clerical help in one of the offices. The satisfaction of participating with your neighbors in a worthy cause will far outweigh the time and energy you devote.

THE JEWISH COMMUNITY   Jewish philanthropies in most large cities will be incorporated in some federated "chest" like the Federation of Jewish Philanthropies in New York City. In some places, fund raising is handled by several organizations grouped in a community council.

All over the United States, you will hear of the annual campaign for the United Jewish Appeal. These drives have special women's divisions. In addition to what your husband gives, respond to these appeals by your own personal contribution.

Your support will be asked, too, for other agencies and causes. For example, in the educational field, American Friends of the Hebrew University, Brandeis University and the Albert Einstein College of Medicine raise funds through women's groups. Your Sisterhood will have fund raising campaigns usually arranged through luncheons, theater parties and other functions. In the Conservative movement, one of the major undertakings of the Women's League (a national Sisterhood organization) is the Torah Fund. In supporting this, you help the Jewish Theological Seminary as well as the educational facilities of your own synagogue. Various membership groups raise funds for their own projects.

BONDS WITH ISRAEL   Don't consider the purchase of Israel Bonds as philanthropy, since this is a financial investment. The Israel Bond organization has a very active women's division with which you may want to work.

THE ORGANIZATION WOMAN

INNUMERABLE NATIONAL JEWISH ORGANIZATIONS feature philanthropic, cultural, educational, religious, mutual benefit, political, social, social welfare, Zionist, pro-Israel or overseas programs. Some of the national women's organizations (listed alphabetically) are: American Jewish Congress Women's Division, B'nai B'rith Women, Hadassah (Women's Zionist Organization), Mizrachi Women's Organization of America, National Council of Jewish Women, Pioneer Women (Women's Labor Zionist Organization of America), Women's American ORT (Organization for Rehabilitation through Training); and national Sisterhood organizations—Women's League for Conservative Judaism (Conservative), Women's Branch of the Union of Orthodox Jewish Congregations of America (Orthodox) and National Federation of Temple Sisterhoods (Reform).

This listing is by no means all-inclusive. For a complete, classified listing, see the *American Jewish Yearbook* published annually by the American Jewish Committee and the Jewish Publication Society of America. It is available in most libraries. You can get helpful information and literature from the national offices of any of the organizations listed; better still, find out through your local chapter.

Working for a Jewish woman's organization not only enables you to perform the mitzvah of service, but offers many personal benefits to you. All these organizations are noted for their excellent educational and cultural programs; for their awareness of what is happening on the political, economic and cultural level in the United States, in Israel and in the United Nations. They frequently arrange trips to the United Nations, the Jewish Museum and other places of interest.

The varied projects of these organizations will make use of any aptitude or skill you may have—organizational ability, leadership, typing, driving, cake baking, sewing or selling. Any creative talent you have in singing, writing, acting, arts or crafts will find a ready outlet here.

Jewish women's organizations give you an opportunity to serve important causes in a friendly, congenial environment.

LET YOUR VOICE BE HEARD In a well-balanced life, you will want to take part in community activities that are not specifically Jewish. You might want to join a local civic group. The parents' association of your children's public school and Hebrew school both deserve your active support and participation. Local hospitals may require volunteer help.

The League of Women Voters and the United Nations Association—for the United States of America are nonpartisan organizations that develop a better understanding of current legislative issues and of world events. In fact, what you learn in the League or the UNA-USA might help you carry the chairmanship of American Affairs, Zionist Affairs or International Relations in your Sisterhood, Hadassah, National Council of Jewish Women, ORT or other group. Even more important, you can serve as the instrument for the presentation of a Jewish point of view in a situation that calls for it. Social action is a basic part of Jewish thinking.

FOR YOUR HUSBAND

SINCE YOU ARE LIKELY to have more leisure time than your husband, show consideration for him. Don't crowd your social calendar to such an extent that he isn't free to attend the meetings of the synagogue, the men's club, the Zionist organization or other service groups. You will both enjoy the stimulation of exchanging news and views about your respective activities.

THE APPLE DOESN'T FALL FAR . . .

YOUR CHILDREN GET THE HABIT of giving and community responsibility from the examples they see at home. In addition, they can learn specifically how to take part in community fund raising through the Keren Ami (Fund of My People), a special project found in many Jewish schools, camps and centers.

Through this project, children and young people learn to give by making regular weekly contributions, and also by giving on special occasions such as holidays and birthdays.

Encourage your youngsters to join some Jewish youth group. Most national Jewish organizations have youth divisions; for example, the Synagogue Youth Groups (page 168), Young Judea, Junior Hadassah, B'nai B'rith Youth Organization.

WHEN PROBLEMS ARISE

THE JEWISH FAMILY has access to excellent social services. If you know of friends or members of the family with problems that cannot be handled by private individuals or agencies, for economic or other reasons, refer them to the Jewish Federation or Jewish Community Service in your town. Jewish social service agencies encompass resources for child care, old age problems, physical or mental illness, marriage counselling.

Take your place in the Jewish and general community to whatever extent you can. As the rabbis have told us, the world rests upon three things—upon *"torah, avodah, gemilut ḥasadim"* ("education, service and good deeds").

CHAPTER 15

Family Fun

"How good and how pleasant it is for brethren to dwell together" (Psalms 133:1)

15

Family Fun

IN THE JEWISH HOME, there are varied opportunities for family fun. This doesn't mean that recreation should be restricted to Jewish activities. You'll find general information on books, music, games, trips and vacations readily available elsewhere, so suggestions given here are mostly limited to areas of Jewish interest.

You and your husband can explore new horizons with the rest of the family. When they "want to know," you can lead them to the appropriate sources and books.

THERE'S NO PLACE LIKE HOME

STAYING HOME can be lots of fun. Even TV and radio can bring the family together instead of isolating its members. Informative and stimulating programs like "Directions" and "The Eternal Light" can be appreciated by the whole family.

The daily newspaper radio and television columns and *TV Guide* list interviews with famous Jewish personalities, preholiday programs and presentations about Israel.

LET THERE BE MUSIC

YOU DO NOT NEED HI-FI or stereophonic equipment to enjoy good music. Building a record library is an exciting family project. A first-class library includes, of course, classics of general interest, some of the good Broadway musicals, perhaps, and other recordings with special appeal to various members of the family. In the Jewish home, in addition, there will be recordings of music on Jewish themes, folk songs, and of the music being composed in Israel today. There will be music by Jewish composers, performances by great Jewish artists, and by the Israeli Symphony Orchestra. A documentary such as *Israel Reborn*, a record of Israel's first decade, gains in significance through the years. Recordings of the Bible read by Abba Eban and by actors and actresses, e.g., Charles Laughton, Judith Anderson, Claire Bloom, are worth owning.

The list which begins on this page is by no means an exhaustive guide, but merely a sampling to show the infinite variety of available records. Record dealers issue extensive catalogs which give alphabetical and classified listings.

A helpful guide to music for the family, and a list of suggestions for gifts, will be found in Eric Werner's *Reviews of Selected Recordings of Jewish Music* (National Jewish Welfare Board).

❦ THE BIBLE IN MUSIC
Handel, ISRAEL IN EGYPT. Oratorio. Angel 3550-B
Mendelssohn, ELIJAH. London A-4315
Copeland, IN THE BEGINNING. Music Library 7007
Tansman, ISAIAH THE PROPHET. Epic LC 3298
Walton, BELSHAZZAR'S FEAST. Westminster WL 5248

❦ RELIGIOUS MUSIC
Bloch, SACRED SERVICE. London 5006
Milhaud, SACRED SERVICE. Concert Hall 1103
Rossi, THE MUSIC OF ROSSI. Columbia ML-5204

❦ FOLK SONG
YIDDISH

THEODOR BIKEL SINGS YIDDISH SONGS. Electra
YIDDISH LOVE SONGS, Ruth Rubin. Riverside RLP 12-647
MARTHA SCHLAMME SINGS JEWISH FOLK SONGS. Vangard VR-S9011
YIDDISH AND HEBREW

JAN PIERCE SINGS HEBREW MELODIES. RCA Victor LM2034

FROM THE HEART OF A PEOPLE, Emma Schaver. Mercury 20052
ANTHOLOGY OF JEWISH SONG, Sylvia Schwartz. Classic 1036
LADINO
  SEPHARDIC SONGS, Gloria Levy. Folkways 8737
HEBREW SONGS
  ISRAELI FOLK DANCES. Israel Music Foundation LP 5
  ISRAELI DANCES. Arzi Records 204
  SONGS OF SONGS, Naomi Zuri. Arzi Records 202
  SHARONA ARON SINGS ISRAELI SONGS. Angel 65018
  SING, ISRAEL, Moshe Nathanson. Metro LP1
  THEODOR BIKEL SINGS SONGS OF ISRAEL. Electra 132
  SUNG BY THE POMEGRANATE TREE, Hillel and Aviva. Concert Hall
  CHS-1228
  SHALOM! ORANIM ZABOR ISRAELI TROUPE. Electra 146
  ON THE ROAD TO ELATH. Oranim Zabor Israeli Troupe. Electra 156
  YEMENITE AND OTHER SONGS, Geula Gill. Folkways.
  MODZITSER MELAVE MALKE MELODIES. Neginah Records, NR1

❧ INSTRUMENTAL MUSIC
Bloch, SCHELOMO RHAPSODY. (A number of excellent recordings.)
Bloch, ISRAEL SYMPHONY. Litschauer, Vienna State Orchestra. Vangard 423
Bernstein, JEREMIAH SYMPHONY. Bernstein, Schyler Symphony Orchestra. Camden 196
Ben Haim, CONCERTO GROSSO FOR STRING ORCHESTRA. Ixler Solomon, MGM Orchestra. MGM-E3423
——, SONATA FOR PIANO. Menahem Pressler. MGM-E3244
——, SUITE FOR PIANO. OP. 34, Bar Ilan. Kingsway 211
Boskovich, SEMITIC SUITE. Rigai, Music Library. MLR 7083
Lavry, FIVE COUNTRY DANCES. Rigai, Music Library. MLR 7083

❧ THE SPOKEN WORD
WORLD OF SHOLOM ALECHEM. Tikva T-28
THE HEBREW LANGUAGE. Theodore Gaster. Folkways FP97-4

❧ CANTORIAL MUSIC
THE ART OF CANTOR JOSEF ROSENBLATT, sung by Josef Rosenblatt. Camden
CANTORIAL MASTERPIECES, sung by Maurice Ganchoff. Tikva

Someone in the family may play the piano or some other instrument. The recorder, a flute-like instrument, is especially suited to family ensemble, and requires little training. In Israel, it is called the *halil*. There are soprano, alto, tenor and bass recorders available. This is an excellent way to study and enjoy Jewish and modern Israeli music. Popular and classical sheet music from Israel can be obtained through SESAC.

There are many occasions at home, or on outings, picnics and trips, for family group singing. The National Jewish Welfare Board, 15 East 26th Street, New York, N. Y. 10010, and the National Jewish Music Council at the same address have prepared excellent material for family music pleasure. They have suggestions for songs and rounds in which the whole family can join, and material on musical games, rhythm bands and family concerts. Just write them for information.

Teen-agers as well as adults can use their talents in writing lyrics and music with Jewish themes for holidays and family events, or in writing new words to familiar music.

Several excellent books on Jewish music are available. See the suggestions on page 199 for books on the history of Jewish music, on folk music, music of the synagogue, and music of modern Israel.

Music is part of the religious experience of the Jews. The beautiful Psalm 150 tells us:

"Hallelujah
Praise God in His Sanctuary. . . .
Praise Him with the harp and lyre.
Praise Him with the drum and dance;
Praise Him with strings and the flute.
Praise Him with the loud-sounding cymbals. . . .
Hallelujah."

On Shabbat and the festivals, the family likes to sing together. The inclusion of *zemirot*, Friday night songs, as part of the Sabbath meal, shows that the Jewish people have long been aware of the importance of song as a family activity.

SHALL WE DANCE?   The serious study of the dance may be for especially talented youngsters, but all the family can enjoy square dancing and Israeli folk dancing in organized groups, or with friends in the home recreation room.

PROGRAM NOTES The Jewish field abounds in possibilities for cultural enrichment. Your daily newspaper will indicate when Israeli musicians, singers or dancers are performing in your community, and when works by Jewish composers or of historic Jewish interest are being played. Exhibits of the work of Israeli artists are shown fairly often through the United States. *The National Jewish Post and Opinion* has an excellent column which lists lectures, symposiums, art exhibits, special events in the theater, and other current activities of interest to Jewish families. The Young Men's Hebrew Association, Lexington Avenue at 92nd Street, is noted for its dance recitals, poetry readings and concerts.

FAMILY READING

THE OLD-FASHIONED CUSTOM of reading aloud is being revived from the platform and on the air. Try reading aloud at home. You might start with simple children's stories. *Pathways Through the Bible,* by Mortimer J. Cohen, (Jewish Publication Society) is suitable for older girls and boys. The family together might read material on the Jewish holidays as they approach. A family fun project could be reading about places and people in anticipation of a trip or vacation.

Reading alone also gives opportunity for reaching out, for pleasant recreation, for growth. Your center or synagogue library will have many of the books you want; some will be available in your local or town library.

GAMES ARE GOOD Very young children have been given special consideration by book publishers and game manufacturers. Besides the many handsome, illustrated books of Jewish content, there are coloring books, cutouts, quizzes and puzzles about the holidays, the Bible and Israel which are both amusing and educational. They include many do-it-yourself activities for holiday preparation. Checkers and chess are good family games since they can be enjoyed by everyone, even on the Sabbath. Check with your Sisterhood book or gift shop for further suggestions.

WHAT'S YOUR HOBBY?

EVERYONE FROM THE PRESCHOOL CHILD to the senior citizen is encouraged by modern physicians and psychologists to develop a hobby. Very often, general interests and creative talents may be directed through specific Jewish areas of interest in writing, art, dramatics, choral work.

Photography, for example, can be channeled to include items of Jewish significance. Holiday scenes make good camera subjects. Jewish ceremonial objects offer unlimited opportunities for artistic still-life photography.

STAMP COLLECTING   Stamp and coin collecting fascinates most boys and girls. Israel issues unusually attractive ones that are rich in history.

Israel, published by Minkus Publishing Company, 116 West 32nd Street, New York, N. Y. 10001, and distributed by Grosset and Dunlop, is a complete, fully illustrated stamp album, with annual supplements. *The History of Israel's Postage Stamps* by Harold U. Ribalow (Twayne Publishing Company) gives interesting background material for the collector.

The Youth Department of the Jewish Agency has a stamp service available to Jewish youth organizations and schools. It issues a bulletin full of fascinating information called *Israel Stamp Workshop.* A catalog published by the Israel Post Office is available free to collectors, by writing to "Philatelic Services, General Post Office, Jerusalem, Israel."

Gimbels Department Store in New York probably has the largest collection of Israel stamps and coins in the world. If your local dealer cannot help you, you can certainly write to Gimbels Stamp Department, Broadway and 33rd Street, New York, N. Y., for information.

A collection of Israeli coins might lead to a study of ancient coins. The modern coins of Israel are beautifully designed, especially the first commemorative coin for the young republic's historic tenth anniversary. For buying this and other coins, the collector will find helpful the *Catalog of Modern World Coins* by R. S. Yeoman (Whitman Publishing Company).

ARTS AND CRAFTS Arts and crafts constitute a rich field for Jewish expression. Teachers have pointed out that through the different arts history becomes a vivid experience. Puppetry, for example, expands language abilities. Right at home, children can make puppets for a "Purim Shpiel" (play) or dress dolls of many nations; they can model Biblical characters in clay or copy the animals of Noah's ark in play-dough. The young girl can embroider a hallah or matzah cover, a holiday tablecloth, a *tallit* bag for her father or brother, or samplers with Shabbat or holiday themes.

Any of the Jewish holidays offer colorful material for decorations or gifts. Tamima Gezari, teacher and authority on Jewish art, has designed a wonderful set of *Art Craft Guides,* which give clear instructions for making a menorah, greeting cards, figurines, and many other articles in different media. These cost only $1.00 for the set and can be obtained by writing to the Jewish Education Committee, New York. In large cities and towns, you might try specialty arts and crafts stores for a more complete selection of materials and suggestions than is usually stocked in the ordinary toy shop.

DO-IT-YOURSELF In Jewish community centers, synagogues, schools and museums it is very easy for the entire family to try its collective hand at ceramics, painting, carpentry, photography, embroidered samplers, beaten copper, leathercraft, mosaics, or sculpture; and to raise its collective voice in choral and dramatic groups.

Organized activity, often free or for a nominal fee, is so planned that both young people and adults can participate. There is a very special satisfaction for a father and son in building and designing a set of bookshelves or for mother and daughter to act together in a community play.

SPORTS The future trophy winner will enjoy Harold U. Ribalow's *The Jew in American Sports* (Bloch Publishing Company). If your center or Hebrew school conducts a "Maccabiad" or field day, on Lag Ba'Omer, encourage your children to participate.

ANTIQUE HUNTERS If you cannot pass an antique shop without stopping, develop a specialty in antique-hunting. Try to find old Jewish ceremonial pieces, but be on guard for forgeries or reproductions that are not authentic.

FOR THAT GREEN THUMB The "green thumb" members of your family might find the following suggestion a challenge: Devote a section of the garden to plants mentioned in the Bible which can be grown in your area, or to plants with Biblical folk names. Even a few house plants chosen from this viewpoint would be fun. Charming articles by Sadie Rose Weilerstein on this subject appeared in the summer and September 1958 issues of *Outlook*. Write to its publisher, the Women's League for Conservative Judaism, 48 E. 74th Street, New York, N. Y. 10021 for back copies.

Just think of the possibilities in combining Bible study with the science of horticulture. Before long, the whole family will join in tracking down the rose of Sharon, Solomon's-seal, Moses-in-the-Bulrushes, or Job's-tears.

THE WORLD IS YOURS

IT IS FUN TO DISCOVER all the exciting places to see in the area in which you live or visit, although we are going to mention particularly those of Jewish interest. You will be surprised to find how many landmarks there are throughout the United States, even in remote villages. For a complete listing and description, see *A Jewish Tourist's Guide* by Bernard Postal and Lionel Koppman (Jewish Publication Society). Though this book will be found in many libraries, it is well worth owning.

BE PREPARED   Preparation for a trip, whether it's a morning visit to a museum or library, or an extended vacation, is important. This check list may be helpful:

Get some background on what you are going to see by reading about it in advance.

Check the exact address and travel directions.

Avoid disappointment by determining exact visiting days and hours.

Dress appropriately.

Find out about eating facilities.

Don't plan to do too much at one time.

Be sure the trip is of interest to all the family members going.

INVEST IN THESE

Reading about your trips in advance, taking pictures when you can, and making a scrapbook afterwards prolong the pleasure of your experience.

Besides the *Jewish Tourist's Guide,* and the Davis map mentioned on page 14, here are some other helpful publications:

TRIP GUIDE TO PLACES OF JEWISH INTEREST IN NEW YORK can be purchased from the National Jewish Welfare Board.

TRIPS FOR CHILDREN—a pamphlet published by the Play Schools Association Inc., 111 East 59th Street, New York, N. Y. 10022.

KID STUFF IN NEW YORK STATE—available free from State Department of Commerce, 112 State Street, Albany, N. Y. Lists children's attractions throughout New York State.

Free descriptive literature and sightseeing information is available on request from the Official Visitor Information Center of the New York Convention and Visitors Bureau, 90 East 42nd Street, New York   N. Y.

Most states and many cities supply helpful literature on their points of interest.

LET'S VISIT NEW YORK CITY

SINCE IT WOULD BE IMPOSSIBLE within the confines of this chapter to list all the places in the United States worth visiting, we are mentioning only some in New York City, with the hope that, if you don't live there, you will sometime visit. Even if you never get to New York, the kinds of trips described here may suggest similar visits near your home.

New York City is a wonderland for children and adults. Many excursions cost nothing at all; others require modest fees. To get an overall picture of this great metropolis, the boat trip around Manhattan might be a good place to start. The Staten Island ferry trip, from which you view the Statue of Liberty, should not be missed. Visits to various sections of the city to see the colorful ethnic and national groups furnish a lesson in geography and history.

The United Nations is a must for every member of the family. Its handsome buildings occupy a six-block area from First Avenue to the East River between 42nd Street and 48th Street. By all means pay the small fee for a conducted tour of the beautiful assembly rooms. Adults and older children can sit in on sessions open to the public. The International Gift Shop in the lower lounge includes items made in Israel.

When Israeli ships dock, you can visit them if you get passes in advance. This is true, incidentally, of other steamship lines. The usual charge is a contribution of fifty cents which goes to the Seaman's Fund. Check with the American-Israeli Shipping Company, 1 World Trade Center, to determine when visitors are allowed.

Airports like La Guardia Field and John F. Kennedy International Airport give you a feeling of traveling to far places. Kennedy Airport is the location of the International Synagogue Center. Here, too, is the artistically designed area of the El Al Israel Airlines terminal. You might also stop at the El Al offices at 850 Third Avenue, New York City, to pick up their travel folders. If you are lucky, they will on request give you some of their posters, which make attractive playroom decorations.

The office of the Consulate General of Israel and the Delegation of Israel to the United Nations at 800 Second Avenue is worth stopping in to see. Incidentally, the consular buildings of many nations in New York City have home product exhibits in their reception rooms. They welcome visitors.

MUSEUM ROW The Jewish Museum on Fifth Avenue and 92nd Street deserves many visits. Watch for its special exhibits; visit its Junior Gallery. Often the exhibits are dioramas created by children, -which can be manipulated by the young visitor. Since this is located in the "Museum Row" section of New York, you might combine a trip to the Jewish Museum with a visit to the Metropolitan Museum of Art on Fifth Avenue and 82nd Street. This, too, has a Junior Museum. The younger children in the family won't want to miss the zoo in Central Park at 65th Street. And don't overlook the Museum of Natural History right across the park from the Metropolitan Museum.

SEMINARY AND SYNAGOGUES The Jewish Theological Seminary on Broadway at 122nd Street is the headquarters for Conservative Judaism. It is in the heart of a cultural center, with Columbia University, Barnard College, Manhattan School of Music among the buildings nearby. The Seminary includes a library which houses the largest collection of Judaica and Hebraica in the world.

Yeshiva University, 186th Street and Amsterdam Avenue, is a famous center for the training of Orthodox rabbis.

At some time, certainly, you will want to visit famous synagogues. Congregation Shearith Israel at Central Park West and 70th Street is the synagogue of the oldest Jewish congregation in North America. It is famous for its collection of ancient ceremonial objects. This congregation is also known as the Spanish and Portuguese Synagogue. Its service is still carried out in the Sephardic tradition.

Temple Emanu-El at Fifth Avenue and 65th Street is a place of worship for Reform Jews, famous for its architectural design and for its magnificent interior, as well as for the Irving Lehman collection of Judaica. Across the street from Temple Emanu-El at 838 Fifth Avenue is the House of Living Judaism, the home of the Union of American Hebrew Congregations (Reform). Its inscriptions, festival plaques and window panels make a visit worth planning.

OF SPECIAL INTEREST   Young and old alike will enjoy a trip to a matzah factory. Call the main office of any of the big companies for details on arrangements. There are many places you may want to visit because of your special organizational work, for example, Hadassah House. All organizational headquarters are listed in the *Jewish Tourist's Guide,* which has a comprehensive index as well as individual descriptions arranged by state and city.

In visiting places of general interest, in New York City or elsewhere, note points of Jewish significance. For example, in the not-to-be-missed visit to the Statue of Liberty, you will be reminded that the poem, "The New Colossus," inscribed on the statue, was written by Emma Lazarus, the great Jewish humanitarian and poetess. The lines are familiar to every school child:

> *Give me your tired, your poor,*
> *Your huddled masses yearning to breathe free. . . .*

While visiting the New York Public Library on Fifth Avenue at 42nd Street, don't miss the room set aside entirely for Judaica.

VACATION GUIDE

VACATION TRIPS by car, bus, train, boat, or plane give you the privilege of being a good-will ambassador for the Jewish people wherever you may go.

Just as you carry with you an automobile club directory or a similar guide to hotels, motels and restaurants, carry the *Jewish Tourist's Guide* mentioned earlier. When you turn to your tour book or guide map for places to visit, don't overlook this book for suggestions about places of Jewish interest. That landmarks, monuments, statues and institutions exist even in out-of-the-way places comes as a pleasant surprise to many travelers.

The *Jewish Travel Guide,* a directory of world travel issued annually by the *London Jewish Chronicle* offers helpful advice to those who travel abroad. This pocket-size book lists synagogues, kashrut arrangements, hotels, restaurants, summer schools and communal organizations all over the world.

Some time, perhaps you will be able to take a trip to Israel, a land that evokes rapturous praise from the most sophisticated travelers. Such a trip is an historic experience. Travel agents can, of course, help you plan an individual trip, but many Jewish organizations arrange special pilgrimages which have the advantage of reduced fees and expertly guided tours.

PEN POINTERS Your children may spend their vacations in summer camps or visiting out-of-town. The child away from home can be drawn into the family circle by mail—not by letters saying how much they are missed, but, rather, by writing of some incident which evokes a picture of the Jewish home scene. A mother might write, "I'm about to light the Shabbat candles. I think about you and your Friday night songs in camp."

Good Jewish living can extend its influence far beyond the walls of home.

HELPFUL REFERENCES FOR THE FAMILY BOTH IN THE GENERAL AND IN THE JEWISH FIELD

✤ ON MUSIC

MUSIC IN THE HOME by Leah M. Jaffa (National Jewish Welfare Board). An outline of Jewish music program suggestions for the family to enjoy together. Sent free on request.

REVIEWS OF SELECTED RECORDINGS OF JEWISH MUSIC by Eric Werner (National Jewish Music Council). Representative and recommended recordings are described and reviewed by experts. Covers children's records, folk and art music as well as music of the synagogue.

✤ FOR THE SONGS THEMSELVES

THE SONGS WE SING by Harry Coopersmith (United Synagogue of America). Music and lyrics for synagogue service; for Sabbath and holidays. Attractive format, illustrated.

THE GATEWAY TO JEWISH SONG by Judith K. Eisenstein (Behrman House). Holiday, ceremonial, Israeli, everyday songs for children. Attractive, illustrated.

SONGS TO SHARE by Rose B. Goldstein (United Synagogue Commission on Jewish Education). Twenty-four songs with piano accompaniment to help the child from three to seven join in family singing.

TREASURY OF JEWISH FOLKSONG by Ruth Rubin (Schocken, hardcover and paperback folio). A good book for a family sing. Illustrated.

SONGS OF CHILDHOOD by Judith Eisenstein and Frieda Prensky (United Synagogue Commission on Jewish Education).

SONGS FOR FUN, vols. I and II, by Ray Cook (Union of American Hebrew Congregations).

✹ ON THE DANCE

JEWISH FOLK DANCE RESOURCES by Leah M. Jaffa (National Jewish Welfare Board). Gives a comprehensive and descriptive list of folk dance books.

DANCES OF THE JEWISH PEOPLE by Dvora Lapson (Jewish Education Committee of New York). The music and words of songs, and careful directions for twenty-seven Israeli and east European dances.

DANCES THE YEAR ROUND by Dvora Lapson (Jewish Education Committee of New York). For special occasions.

JEWISH FOLK DANCE BOOK by Katya Delakova and Fred Berk (National Jewish Welfare Board). Discusses the influences in the development of the Jewish folk dance, and gives instructions for several dances.

JEWISH HOLIDAY DANCES by Corinne Chochen (Behrman House). Illustrations and directions for festival folk dances.

✹ ON OTHER INTERESTS

A PARENT'S GUIDE TO CHILDREN'S READING by Nancy Larrick (Doubleday). Pointers on reading aloud to children, selecting books for children, helping them choose books for themselves.

FOOTPRINTS AND NEW WORLDS by Temima Gezari (Reconstructionist Press). Description of creative experiences in art with children and adults, in general as well as Jewish education. Good chapter on museum tours.

THE JEW IN AMERICAN SPORTS by Harold U. Ribalow (Bloch Publishing Company). The personality sketches and anecdotes of about thirty American-Jewish athletes—in baseball, football, boxing, basketball, golf, tennis and other sports.

PLANTS OF THE BIBLE by A. W. Anderson (Crosby Lockwood and Sons, Ltd., London). This unusual book gives Bible quotations and descriptions of plants mentioned in the Bible. It has full-page pictures of the plants in color. An attractive gift book.

THE BIBLICAL ZOO written and illustrated by Susan Nevil (McKay).

✹ ON TRIPS AND TRAVEL

A JEWISH TOURIST'S GUIDE TO THE UNITED STATES by Bernard Postal and Lionel Koppman (Jewish Publication Society). Vast amount of information. Points of Jewish interest throughout the

United States classified by state, and indexed alphabetically. Of interest both to traveler and stay-at-home.

JEWISH TRAVEL GUIDE issued annually by the *London Jewish Chronicle* (American agent, Bloch Publishing Company). Lists synagogues, kashrut facilities, hotels, restaurants, summer schools, organizations, travel agencies all over the world. Special sections on United States and Israel. Pocket size.

❧ SOME GENERAL BOOKS ON FAMILY FUN

THE HAPPY HOME—A Guide to Family Living by Agnes E. Benedict and Adele Franklin (Appleton-Century-Crofts, Inc.). Chapters on family activity—conversation, work and play, festivities, trips, creative growth, vacations.

HAVE FUN WITH YOUR CHILDREN by Frances R. Horwich and Reinald Werrenrath, Jr. (Prentice-Hall). Suggestions for creative activities.

NOTE: The National Recreation Association, 8 West 8th Street, New York   N. Y., has a good general listing of books on home play, special celebrations, music, arts and crafts, games, etc. List free on request.

Many of the gasoline companies supply free helpful booklets on traveling with children, and places to visit.

CHAPTER 16

Making the Most of Your Money

"*Where there is no bread, there is no Torah;*
If there is no Torah, there is no bread" (*Pirke Avot*)

.

— 16 —

Making the Most of Your Money

W HAT IS A CHAPTER on budgeting doing in a book for the Jewish homemaker? Part of the answer can be found in the quotation on page 203. Our tradition recognizes that both material and spiritual needs must be fulfilled for members of the family to lead happy, full lives.

DOLLARS AND SENSE

THIS, OF COURSE, does not imply that wealth necessarily means happiness. The amount of money you have is of secondary importance; knowing what you want to do with it is essential. This matter requires more than arithmetic or the making of lists and charts. These will be needed, but first there must be an understanding and agreement between husband and wife on their basic philosophy, values and beliefs.

MAN-TO-WOMAN TALK The money problem, unfortunately, often looms early in married life. The trouble is not usually the amount of money, but how it's to be spent and who will handle it. A heart-to-heart, or better, perhaps, a head-to-head talk between husband and wife early in their marriage, anticipating the difficulties rather than waiting till they arise, will save many a painful scene.

When there are only two of you, long-term goals undoubtedly include home furnishings, job improvement, study or travel. Short term goals perhaps take into account new clothing, a library of Judaica, records, some Jewish festival accessory. After children come, the goals will be multiplied to include provision for education, special schools and camps, and for developing individual talents.

MONEYWISE

IF YOU CONSIDER MONEY only one of the resources which you budget for happy family life, planning its use will be easier. In reality, budgeting is an essential element in living. Consciously or unconsciously, we budget our time and energy as well as our money.

The homemaker plans her schedules to take care of the necessary daily chores, special weekly ones, and occasional seasonal or annual jobs. Time left over or time saved is used for reading and study, recreation, hobbies or community work. In the same way, she cleverly budgets her energy so that after the cleaning and cooking, she has time left for playing with her children or being a companion to her husband. In getting ready for the Sabbath or a holiday, for example, don't use up all your energy so that none is left for enjoying the happy day.

Similarly, money is budgeted so that first the basic needs such as rent, food and clothing are taken care of, and then the other items. Money is the simplest resource to budget since it is the most tangible.

A budget cannot spend or save money for you; it cannot produce money that doesn't exist. But it can help you keep track of your finances and guide the way you spend and save for maximum family happiness. A simple budget is easy to set up. The important thing is to plan it realistically and to keep it.

A MODEL BUDGET The sample budget which follows is just a suggestion. Work out one that suits your needs best and makes for the easiest bookkeeping for you. In the budget for almost any Jewish home, philanthropy (contributions) and education are two items that are considered fixed expenses, just as are rent or taxes.

Many of us remember from childhood the charity coin box that was as much a part of the kitchen as the egg beater or the chopping knife. No matter how modest the home, a penny or two regularly found its way into the charity box, usually before the lighting of the candles on the Sabbath eve.

TZEDAKAH AND TAXES To turn from *tzedakah* (equitable giving) or philanthropy to income tax may seem an unrelated step. In reality, it is logical to think of them together. The United States government recognizes the virtue of charitable contributions by allowing a considerable deduction for them on your income tax.

Keep an accurate record of your contributions, including check stubs and receipts. Deductions are allowed not only for outright cash giving, but for use of a car for fund raising; for clothing or other items given to rummage sales or bazaars, if the value can be estimated.

Trust funds, long-term gifts, or money bequests to philanthropic, educational or medical organizations are tax deductible. This subject is too complex for detailed discussion here; consult a lawyer or accountant for specific advice.

A MODEL BUDGET
Estimate of Total Income

Annual wages and/or—
Income from Business or Profession
Interest or Dividends from Bonds and Investments
Other Income

Total Annual Income ....
(divide by 52 for weekly budget or by 12 for monthly budget)

Estimate of Expenses

Item	Annual	Weekly or Monthly

Fixed Expenses

Rent or mortgage payment
Taxes
Social Security
Insurance
  Life
  Health and Hospital
  Other
Dues or fees—union or professional; synagogue, organizations
Education—Jewish education as well as college; music, art, etc.
Contributions—to synagogue, Israel, Jewish causes, local charities,
  national drives
Emergency Fund

Semi-fixed Expenses

Food—including holiday delicacies, special foods as at Passover
Household operating—gas, electricity, fuel, telephone, laundry,
  repairs, help
Clothing
Transportation—including car, if you own one

Variable Expenses

Additional education items—general and Jewish
Recreation
Books, newspapers, magazines—including Jewish books, magazines,
  pictures, art objects
Gifts
Hobbies
Vacations
Holidays—including observance of Sabbath and Jewish holidays
  and customs

Savings

For short- and long-term goals

FAMILY FINANCE

FAMILY FINANCE doesn't end with the budget; it really begins there. The homemaker should be familiar with many other phases of money management. Here we will simply call attention to them, and suggest that you refer to the books listed on page 215 for further explanation.

A reliable investment counsellor, an official of your bank or its trust department will always be glad to discuss special problems with your husband and you.

Ask about these:

Savings accounts	Life insurance
Stocks, other securities	Disability insurance
United States Bonds	Hospital & medical insurance
Israel Bonds	Other insurance
Real estate	Unemployment insurance

Workmen's compensation
Social Security
Veteran's benefits

Record pertinent information in a notebook, indicating location of items, description, certificate numbers, and documents to establish ownership, if necessary.

SAFE DEPOSIT   Store in a safe place records, valuables and important papers. An inexpensive metal box for home use can be purchased, or a safe deposit box in a bank vault rented for bonds, stock certificates, photostats of birth certificates or other important records.

WHAT EVERY WOMAN SHOULD KNOW   It is difficult for a young, happy, healthy married couple to think in terms of the time when prolonged illness, disability or death may come. But while both husband and wife are young and well is exactly the time to look ahead.

If you, aren't already familiar with routine family money matters, start to learn now. Learn how to handle checks properly and how to make out an income tax form. Check with your lawyer on what should be in whose name.

"THE MEMORY OF THE RIGHT-
EOUS IS A BLESSING" PROVERBS 10:7

WITH PROFOUND SYMPATHY
AND A HEARTFELT WISH THAT
THE MEMORY OF

MAY FOREVER ENDURE. ETER-
NAL AS THE TORAH. WHICH
EVERLASTINGLY GIVES LIGHT
AND LOVE TO THE WORLD.

A card sent by Women's League to a bereaved family to indicate
that a memorial contribution has been made

WHERE THERE'S A WILL

YOUNG COUPLES MAY BE HESITANT about making wills, but as the family becomes established, and especially where there are children, a lawyer should be consulted. A will must be technically correct to be valid. Wills should be reviewed every five years or so, as your assets and family status change.

Socially conscious people frequently remember worthy causes in their wills. Art objects or a valuable library are sometimes willed to deserving institutions. Philanthropic and service organizations are glad to provide information on monetary or other bequests.

BEQUEST FORM

I hereby give, devise and bequeath to Hadassah Medical Relief Association, Inc. (or to Hadassah, the Women's Zionist Organization of America, Inc.), 65 East 52nd Street, New York 22, N. Y., a New York membership corporation, the sum of $ .... to be used in the furtherance of its work in Israel.

If the benefactor wishes to specify that his bequest be used for a special phase of Hadassah's work, he may add:

— to be used in furtherance of its medical program ...
— to be used in furtherance of its Medical Center building program ...
— to be used in furtherance of its vocational education program ...
— to be used in furtherance of its work for Youth Aliyah ...

Local chapters and groups should not be designated as beneficiaries, since their unincorporated status may cause difficulties in some states.

---

*Attorneys should check provisions of pertinent state probate codes and inheritance laws as to limitations on bequests to charities which may be applicable to Hadassah.

A truly Ethical Will reflects the Character and Moral purposes of its author, and requires Deed as well as Thought. By your Thought, you guide your children in "the way of the Lord" and by your Deed, you demonstrate to them your high evaluation of the good life.

A bequest form available from Hadassah

GENERAL BEQUEST

I give, devise and bequeath to The Jewish Theological Seminary of America, a corporation existing under the laws of the State of New York and located at New York City, in said State, the sum of⎯⎯⎯⎯⎯⎯Dollars (or property, securities, etc. — giving description), (in memory of ⎯⎯⎯⎯⎯⎯⎯⎯⎯⎯ furnishing a name, if desired). for the general purposes of the said Seminary.

BEQUEST TO ESTABLISH ENDOWED SCHOLARSHIP OR AWARD

I give, devise and bequeath to The Jewish Theological Seminary of America, a corporation existing under the laws of the State of New York and located at New York City, in said State, the sum of⎯⎯⎯⎯⎯⎯Dollars (or property, securities, etc.—giving description), to establish an Endowment Fund to be known as "THE⎯⎯⎯⎯⎯⎯⎯⎯⎯ SCHOLARSHIP (or AWARD) FUND," the income of which shall be awarded annually to a deserving student in the Rabbinical School of the said Seminary.

From the pamphlet on wills (including a collection of ethical wills of famous people) published by the Jewish Theological Seminary of America

EXTRACTS FROM THE "ETHICAL WILL"
BY RABBI JUDAH IBN TIBBON
(12TH CENTURY SPAIN)

My son, ability is of no avail without inclination. Exert yourself while young.

Devote yourself to science and religion; accustom yourself to moral living.

There are two sciences, ethics and physics; strive to excel in both.

Take good care of your health; do not be your own destroyer.

Let not prospect of great gain blind you to risk your life. Do not be like a bird that sees the grain and not the net. Respect your family by providing decent clothes according to your means.

My son, show kindness to all human beings. Tend those who are sick and heal the poor gratuitously.

Honor your wife to your utmost capacity.

All I ask of you is to attain a higher degree of wisdom; to behave in a friendly spirit toward all; to gain a good name; to deserve praise for your dealings with your fellow men; to revere God and perform his commandments.

Devote yourself to your children; be tender to them; be not indifferent to any ailment in them or yourself.

Arrange your library in fair order so as not to weary yourself in your search for the book you need. Never refuse to lend books to anyone who can be entrusted to return them.

Honor your teachers and attach yourself to your friends. Treat them with respect in all places and under all circumstances.

LONG LIFE, PEACE AND SUSTENANCE

THE PRAYER FOR THE NEW MOON, which is recited at the beginning of each month in the Jewish calendar, includes among the blessings for long life, health, and peace, the hope for sustenance *(parnassah)*. These blessings are all inclusive. Money, if put in proper perspective, helps to assure a good life, educational and cultural benefits and the mitzvah of giving.

DO take time out for family discussions on money. Teen-agers and even younger children will enjoy helping to decide whether the month's "extra" should go for a new living-room lamp, a new hi-fi recording, or a Synagogue Youth week end.

Give allowances even to the younger children, to teach them how to handle money and make decisions.

Start early to put aside something for at least one trip to Israel.

Check the stationery store or five-and-ten for an inexpensive budget book with space for daily and annual records.

Keep clear records of family finances.

Learn how to balance a checkbook.

Record contributions; file receipts and check stubs.

Learn how to fill out an income tax form.

Find out about social security benefits.

Discuss with your husband and insurance agent a suitable insurance program for your family's needs.

Make sure that you and your husband write out a will jointly or individually and that it is properly filed.

Be advised of family debts, if there are any.

Provide for a family cemetery plot. This can sometimes be done through your synagogue or through a Jewish fraternal organization.

THESE ARE GOOD REFERENCES

❧ ON FAMILY FINANCE AND BUDGETING

MANAGEMENT IN FAMILY LIVING by P. Nickell and J. M. Dorsey (John Wiley & Sons).

MANAGING YOUR MONEY by J. K. Lasser and Sylvia Porter (Henry Holt and Co.)

HOW TO MAKE YOUR BUDGET BALANCE by Helen Fowle and E. C. Howard (Arco Publishing Company, for the American Institute for Economic Research).

❧ ON INCOME TAXES

YOUR INCOME TAX by J. K. Lasser (Simon and Schuster). Information by an expert.

❧ SOME FREE PAMPHLETS

The Institute of Life Insurance (Educational Division), 488 Madison Avenue, New York   N. Y., will send you, on request, two excellent pamphlets on budgeting: "A Date With Your Future" and "The Family Money Manager." The Institute also has a handbook on life insurance as well as free literature giving expert information.

"Your Job and Your Money" is a booklet giving compact information on many aspects of family finances. Write to *Changing Times*, 1729 H Street N.W., Washington, D. C.

NOTE: The Bureau of Internal Revenue publishes annually a simplified version of the tax law which can be purchased from the Superintendent of Documents, Washington, D. C.

Basic Recipes for a Lifetime

". . . a cheerful heart hath a continual feast" (Proverbs 15:15)

— 17 —

Basic Recipes for a Lifetime

THE FAMOUS SECTION of Proverbs which begins "A woman of valour who can find" includes the lines:

> She is like the merchant ships;
> She bringeth her food from afar.
> She riseth also while it is yet night,
> And giveth food to her household. . . .

Although the modern homemaker does not have to rise while it is yet night, she still, in one sense, "bringeth her food from afar." Jewish dishes that are now taken for granted as "traditional" were picked up along the way in many lands in different times as the Jewish people wandered from place to place.

Here in America, Jewish cooking is truly international, traditional, and at the same time, very· contemporary. The modern homemaker has effected a happy blend of Old-World recipes with modern efficient methods. Many mixes, semiprepared foods and frozen foods have preserved some of the flavor of what "mother used to make."

The Jewish culinary heritage is a varied one, enriched by national dishes, folkways and family memories. It is a constantly growing one, as visitors to Israel can testify. Though new recipes are being added all the time, the old well-loved ones continue to give a particular flavor to each holiday.

This chapter is not intended to be a substitute for a cookbook, but it seems in order to include here recipes for some of the traditional dishes and culinary delicacies. You will, no doubt, have many recipes of your own, "aged-in-the-family" specialities or others exchanged with friends and neighbors. At the end of the chapter there is a list of cookbooks for further ideas.

The basic recipes given here are by no means the only traditional ones. These few samples are time tested, simple, easy to follow, and they taste good. They have infinite variations; you may like to experiment on your own.

"To take delight in special dish, roast ducks,
quail and fish" (*Zemirot*)

HALLAH
"Eat thy bread with joy" (Ecclesiastes 9:7)

1 cake or package yeast	2 tsps. salt
2 tsps. sugar	2 eggs
1¼ cups lukewarm water	2 tbsps. salad oil
4½ cups sifted flour	1 egg yolk

4 tbsps. poppy seeds (optional)

Combine the yeast, sugar and ¼ cup of the water and let the mixture stand for 5 minutes. Sift the flour and salt into a bowl, make a well in the center, and drop the eggs, oil, remaining cup of water and yeast mixture into it. Work into the flour. Knead the dough on a floured board until smooth and elastic. Place in a bowl and brush the top with oil. Cover with a towel and set in a warm place to rise for about an hour. Punch the dough down, cover again, and let it rise until double in bulk.

Divide the dough in half.* Then divide each half into three equal parts. Roll these into three strips of equal length between lightly floured hands, and braid the strips together. Taper the ends and press the edges together. Place the 2 loaves in greased baking pans, cover with a towel and let them rise until double in bulk.

Brush the loaves with the egg yolk, and, if desired, sprinkle them with poppy seeds. Bake in a 375° oven for about 45 minutes or until done.

VARIATIONS: Instead of two equal loaves, one large twist can be made and several miniature twists or rolls. For Rosh Hashanah, a round loaf may be formed.

Hallah is one food which may be found in excellent quality in most large metropolitan bakeries.

* Before forming the loaves, take off a small piece of dough, pronounce the benediction (page 244), and burn the portion of dough.

GEFILLTE FISH

This delicacy, which is identified in most American Jewish homes as a Shabbat and holiday dish, is actually of Eastern European origin. Oriental and even many Western European families never serve this dish.

2 pounds whitefish	4 tsps. salt
2 pounds pike	1½ tsps. pepper
2 pounds carp	3 eggs
(or 3 pounds each of any two of these or any other combinations of fresh-water fish obtainable)	¾ cup ice water
	½ tsp. sugar
	3 tbsps. matzah or cracker meal or bread crumbs (fine)
4 medium onions	3 sliced carrots

Fillet the fish (some fish stores will do this for you) and reserve the head, skin and bones. Place the fish trimmings, 3 of the onions, 2 teaspoons of salt and ¾ teaspoon of pepper in 1 quart of water in a saucepan and cook the stock over high heat.

Meanwhile prepare the fish. Grind the fish and remaining onion, place them in a chopping bowl, and add the eggs, ice water, meal, sugar, and remaining salt and pepper. Chop the mixture until very fine and thoroughly blended. Moisten the hands and shape the mixture into balls. Drop the balls gently into the fish stock and add the carrots. Cover the pan loosely and simmer for about 1½ hours. If stock simmers down too low, add a little water. Remove the cover for the last half hour. Adjust the seasoning, if necessary, and cool the fish slightly in the pan. Remove the fish to a bowl, strain the stock over it, and garnish with the carrots. Chill the fish and serve it with grated horseradish. Serves 12.

VARIATION: Fish may be formed into a loaf or mold instead of balls, and baked. May be served hot or cold.

CHOPPED LIVER

1 pound broiled * liver (poultry, beef or calf)	1 or 2 onions, diced
2 to 4 tbsps. chicken fat	3 hard-cooked eggs
	1 tsp. salt

¼ tsp. pepper

Wash the liver after broiling. Heat 2 tablespoons of fat in a skillet and sauté the onions. Reserve the onions and sauté the livers in the remaining fat. Grind or chop the livers, onions and eggs and mix them to a smooth paste. Add the salt and pepper, and additional fat, if desired. Blend the mixture well. Serve on crackers or *matzot*, on lettuce or as a filling for celery stalks.

* See page 22.

TZIMMES

A tzimmes may be almost any combination of meat with fruits or vegetables; or even fruits or vegetables without meat. In cooking any tzimmes, it is important that it be slowly cooked for a long time to get the best blending of flavors. Some variation of this dish is often served on Rosh Hashanah because it is a sweet dish, and therefore symbolic of the wish for a year of sweetness. The fact that it can be completely prepared in advance and kept warm also makes it a good Sabbath and holiday dish.

SWEET POTATO AND PRUNE TZIMMES

1½ lb. prunes	¼ tsp. pepper
3 cups boiling water	5 medium sweet potatoes, cut in coarse pieces
2 tbsps. chicken fat	
3 lb. boneless chuck or brisket	⅓ cup brown sugar or ½ cup honey
1 chopped onion	
1½ tsps. salt	½ tsp. cinnamon

Wash the prunes and soak in boiling water. Melt the fat in a Dutch oven or large, heavy saucepan. Cut the beef in about 8 pieces and brown with the onion. Sprinkle with salt and pepper, cover the pan, and cook over low heat for 1 hour. Add the prunes and the water in which they were soaked, the sweet potatoes, sugar or honey, and cinnamon. Replace the cover loosely and cook over low heat for 2 hours; or place it in a casserole and bake in a 350° oven until the meat is tender. Serves 6-8.

VARIATION: Can be made with carrots substituting for the potatoes or the prunes.

POTATO LATKES

5 large potatoes	1 tsp. baking powder
2 eggs	1 tsp. salt
2 tbsps. flour or 1 tbsp. matzoh meal	Pepper (optional)
	1 small grated onion (optional)

Shortening, as needed, for frying

Peel the potatoes, grate them on a fine grater, and drain off most of the liquid. Beat the eggs and add them to the potatoes. Add the dry ingredients and the onion, if desired, and mix the batter well. Melt the shortening in a skillet and drop the batter by tablespoons into the hot fat. Fry the latkes on both sides until they are brown. Serve them hot with applesauce. Serves 8.

NOTE: May be served with dairy or meat meals, depending on shortening used. For Passover, use matzah meal instead of flour and omit baking powder.

POTATO KUGEL

This is a variant of potato latkes.

3 eggs	½ tsp. baking powder
3 cups grated raw potatoes (5 or 6 potatoes)	1½ tsp. salt
	Dash of pepper
½ cup flour	1 grated onion (optional)

Drain the potatoes. Beat the eggs until they are thick, and stir in the drained potatoes and all the other ingredients. Turn the batter into a well-greased 1½ quart casserole or baking dish. Bake the kugel, uncovered, in a 350° oven for about 1 hour. Serves 6 to 8.

VARIATION: This may be baked in individual muffin tins, instead of one large kugel.

NOTE: For Passover, substitute matzah meal for the flour and potato starch for the baking powder.

KREPLACH

Kreplach are associated with many of the holidays. On Rosh Hashanah, they are often served in the soup; meat kreplach are sometimes served on the day before Yom Kippur, and cheese kreplach are often served on Shavuot.

Prepare the following noodle dough:

1½ cups flour	1 tbsp. water
2 eggs	½ tsp. salt

Place the unsifted flour on a board and make a well in the center. Drop the eggs, water and salt into it, work them into the flour and kneed the dough until it is smooth and elastic. Flour the board lightly and roll out dough to ⅛ inch thickness. Cut the dough into 3-inch squares. Place 1 tablespoon of the desired filling on each square. Fold one corner over diagonally to form a triangle and press the edges together lightly, using a little water to seal them. Cook the kreplach in rapidly boiling salted water or soup for 20 minutes. Serve the kreplach in soup or as a side dish. To serve as a side dish, they may also be browned in the oven. Makes approximately 2 dozen kreplach.

FILLINGS

Approximately 2 cups of filling are required. Your choice of:

Meat (cooled sautéed chopped meat and onions, seasoned)

Kasha (cooked and mixed with sautéed onion and seasoning)

Cottage or *pot cheese* (mixed with egg and seasoning; minced onion and sour cream may also be added)

Potato (mashed and mixed with sautéed onion and seasoning)

NOTE: Filled kreplach (uncooked) may be covered with a damp cloth and refrigerated for several hours; or they may be wrapped in aluminum foil and frozen.

BLINTZES

Prepare the following batter:

3 eggs	1 cup water or milk
½ tsp. salt	1 cup sifted flour
	Shortening for frying

Prepare filling as indicated below, and set it aside.

Beat the eggs, add the salt, water and flour and beat to a smooth batter. Heat shortening in a 6-inch skillet. Drop in just enough batter to make one thin pancake (about 2 tablespoons). Quickly tilt the pan to coat the bottom and fry until the pancake is firm but not brown. Cook on one side only and carefully turn it out of the pan, bottom side up, on a clean cloth or towel. Continue this procedure until all the batter is used up. Place 1 heaping tablespoon of any of the prepared fillings on one end of a pancake and roll it up like a jelly roll. Fry the blintzes in shortening until they are golden brown, or bake them in a 425° oven. Blintzes may be stored in the refrigerator before cooking for later use. Makes about 18 pancakes.

FILLINGS:

The popular cheese filling consists of a mixture of 2 cups cottage cheese, drained, 1 egg, ¾ teaspoon of salt, and either sugar, cinnamon, or lemon juice, if desired.

Other fillings may be blueberry, cherry, or prune mixtures, or even the meat mixture used in kreplach. Serve the cheese or fruit blintzes with sour cream or sugar and cinnamon.

NOODLE CHEESE KUGEL

5 cups cooked noodles	2 cups cottage cheese
3 tbsps. melted shortening	1 tsp. salt
4 eggs	2 tbsps. sugar (optional)
¾ cup sour cream	Dash of cinnamon (optional)

Mix the noodles and shortening, add the other ingredients, and mix thoroughly. If a sweeter pudding is desired, add the sugar and cinnamon. Place the pudding in a greased 2-quart casserole, dot it with butter, or margarine and sprinkle it with bread crumbs, if desired. Bake the pudding in a 350° oven for 40 to 50 minutes. Serves 6 to 8.

VARIATIONS: Raisins, apples, prunes, or nuts may be added. For a meat meal, a noodle pudding must be made with chicken fat or "pareve" margarine or shortening, without the cheese or cream.

FOR PASSOVER

HAROSET

This is one of the ceremonial dishes for the seder.

1 apple, peeled, cored and chopped fine	½ tsp. sugar
½ cup shelled walnuts or pecans, ground or chopped fine	½ tsp. cinnamon
	1 tbsp. kosher red wine

Mix together the apple, nuts, sugar and cinnamon. Add the wine and mix thoroughly. Allow 1 tablespoon of *haroset* per serving.

CHREMSLACH (Matzah Meal Pancakes)

3 eggs (separated)	½ cup cold water
1 tsp. salt	¾ cup matzah meal

Shortening for frying

Beat together the egg yolks, salt and water, and stir in the matzah meal. Beat whites stiff and fold them carefully into the batter. Drop the batter by the tablespoon into hot fat in a skillet. Fry the pancakes until they are light brown on both sides. Chremslach can be served as a side dish with meat, or as a dessert with sugar and cinnamon or jam. Serves 3 or 4.

VARIATIONS: Can be made with fillings; for example, with potatoes as a meat side dish, or with mashed stewed prunes or apricots for dessert.

K'NAIDLACH (Matzah Meal Dumplings)

2 tbsp. chicken fat or other shortening	½ cup matzah meal
	1 tsp. salt
2 eggs, lightly beaten	2 tbsps. water or soup stock

Mix together shortening and eggs, add matzah meal and salt and blend the mixture well. Add water or stock. Cover the mixture and chill it for at least 20 minutes. Form into plum-size balls and drop them gently in boiling salted water or soup. Cook the dumplings for 30 to 40 minutes and serve them in soup. Makes about 16 k'naidlach.

VARIATION: For lighter, fluffier k'naidlach, separate the eggs and beat the yolks and whites separately. Proceed as above, but fold the egg whites into the yolks carefully before adding the matzah meal.

NOTE: During the year, but *not* for Passover, 1 teaspoon of baking powder may be added to this recipe.

MATZAH CHARLOTTE

3 matzot	1 tsp. cinnamon (optional)
4 eggs (separated)	¼ cup shortening
½ cup sugar	Fruit (optional)

Crumble the *matzot* (or matzah "farfel" may be used), soak in cold water until it is soft, and drain. Beat together the egg yolks and sugar, add the *matzot* and the optional ingredients, if desired. Beat the egg whites stiff, fold them in, and turn into a well-greased casserole or baking dish. Dot with shortening and bake in a 350° oven for about 1 hour, or until well browned. Serve the pudding hot. It may be accompanied by stewed fruit, or a fruit or wine sauce. Serves 6 to 8.

VARIATIONS: The fruit added may be diced or grated apple, raisins, grated orange rind, prunes. Even nuts may be added, or add ¼ cup wine for more flavor.

PASSOVER SPONGE CAKE

8 eggs (separated)	Juice of ½ lemon
1½ cups sugar	¼ cup cake flour
Rind of 2 lemons	¾ cup potato starch

¼ tsp. salt

Beat egg whites to form peaks. Beat egg yolks with the sugar, lemon rind and lemon juice until they are almost white and like custard. Sift the cake flour, potato starch and salt. Fold the egg whites and dry ingredients alternately into the yolks. Bake in 2 ungreased layer cake pans in a 325° oven for 1 hour, or until done. Invert pans; hang on funnel or bottle to cool thoroughly.

Israeli Recipe (courtesy of Hadassah)

PAROSA FROM ISRAEL (VIA GREECE)

1 lb. creamed cottage cheese	Dash of salt
2 eggs (separated)	¼ cup plain yoghurt
¼ cup sugar	2 tbsps. melted butter or
½ tsp. cinnamon	margarine

2 tbsps. all-purpose flour

Blend thoroughly the cheese, egg yolks, sugar, cinnamon and salt. Add the yoghurt to make a thick paste. Add the melted butter or margarine. Stir in the flour. Beat the egg whites stiff and fold into the mixture. Pour into a greased quart casserole. Set the casserole into a shallow pan of water and bake uncovered in a 350° oven for 1 hour. Chill. May be served with more yoghurt. Serves 4 to 6.

CAKES

HONEYCAKE

4 eggs	1 tsp. baking soda
1⅓ cups sugar	1 cup coffee (strong)
1 lb. honey	3 tsps. lemon juice
⅜ cup oil	2 tsps. brandy
3⅓ cups flour	1 cup chopped nuts
1⅓ tsps. baking powder	1 cup raisins

Preheat oven to 350°. Mix the eggs and sugar, add the honey, and mix well. Add the oil and blend it well. Sift together the flour, baking powder and baking soda two times, and add this mixture to the egg mixture alternately with the cool coffee. Mix the batter well and add the lemon juice and brandy. Add ¾ cup of chopped nuts and the raisins, and pour the batter into an ungreased 10-inch tube form. Sprinkle ½ cup of nuts over top. Bake the cake at 350° for 1 hour, or until done. Invert immediately to cool and pry the cake out gently with a spatula.

HAMANTASHEN (for Purim)

4 eggs	2 tsps. vanilla
1 cup oil	3 tsps. baking powder
1¼ cups sugar	½ tsp. salt

5½ cups flour (approx.)

Beat eggs, beat in oil, sugar, vanilla, baking powder, salt. Add flour gradually; mix thoroughly. Knead till smooth enough to roll on floured board. Roll out. Cut dough into 3- to 4-inch rounds. Place desired filling on each round. Pinch together sides of lower half of circles to form triangles. Place Hamantashen on a lightly greased baking sheet or pan and bake at 350° for ½ hour, or until golden brown.

FILLINGS

The usual fillings are cooked prunes or mohn (poppyseeds). The prune filling may be made from cooked dried prunes with ground nuts and orange rind added. The prepared baby food prunes may also be used; or the mashed prune filling called "lekva."

NOTE: The above recipe is a useful one because it is "pareve." Almost any yeast dough could be used for hamantashen.

CHEESECAKE

CRUST

1 cup zwieback or graham cracker crumbs	1 tbsp. butter or margarine 1 tbsp. sugar

Blend the mixture and press it into the bottom of a 10-inch springform cake pan.

FILLING

1 lb. cream cheese	2 tbsps. flour
1 cup sugar	Dash of salt
4 eggs (separated)	1 tsp. vanilla

1 cup evaporated milk

Cream the cheese with ¾ cup of sugar, add the egg yolks and blend thoroughly. Add the flour, salt, vanilla, and mix well. Add evaporated milk. Beat the egg whites until foamy, add ¼ cup of sugar and beat the whites until stiff. Fold the whites into the cheese mixture. When all is blended, pour the filling into the lined cake pan.

Bake the cheesecake at 325° for 1 hour or more. Test by touching lightly in the center with your finger. Cake is done when no depression is left.

NUT TORTE

6 eggs (separated)	½ cup matzah meal
1 cup sugar	2 tbsps. cake flour
Juice of ½ lemon	½ tsp. salt
Juice and rind of ½ orange	1 cup walnuts, finely chopped

Beat the egg yolks, add the sugar gradually and beat until the mixture is light in color. Add the lemon juice, the orange juice and rind, and mix in the dry ingredients. Fold in the stiffly beaten egg whites. Bake in an ungreased spring-form cake pan at 350° for 45 minutes, or until the cake tests done. Cool the cake and spread the top and sides with orange icing.

Icing

1 egg white, unbeaten	3 tbsps. orange juice
⅞ cup sugar	½ tsp. grated orange rind

Place all ingredients in the top of a double boiler over boiling water, and beat with an egg beater for 7 minutes. Cool the icing before spreading it on cake.

STRUDEL (Stretched Dough)

3 cups sifted flour	2 eggs
¼ tsp. salt	3 tbsps. salad oil
¼ cup lukewarm water	

Sift together the flour and salt. Combine the eggs, oil and water, and work them into the flour, mixing until the dough leaves the side of the bowl. Knead the dough for about 10 minutes, or until it is smooth. Place a warm bowl over it, and let stand for about 20 minutes.

Cover a large working surface with a clean tablecloth. (A kitchen table about 24 to 30 inches square is about right; you should be able to walk around the table.) Sprinkle the cloth with flour and roll out the dough as thin as you can; be careful not to tear it.

Now begin the stretching process. Flour the knuckles of your hands, form your hands into fists and place them under the pastry. Carefully and gently pull the dough toward you with the back of your hands. Change your position around the table from time to time so that the dough is stretched in all directions without strain. Continue stretching until the dough is transparent and as thin as tissue paper. Cut away any thick edges. Brush with oil or melted shortening.

Place filling down the length of one side about 2 inches in from the edge. Turn this 2-inch flap over the filling and lift the cloth to continue to roll the dough over and over from that edge. Cut rolled strudel down the middle into two loaves. Place the loaves on a heavily greased baking pan, brush the tops with oil, and bake them in a 400° oven for about 35 minutes, or until they are crisp and brown. Cut into slices. Each strudel will yield about 20 slices.

FILLINGS

There are many varieties. Two popular ones are given here.

Apple: Peel, core and chop 4 or 5 apples. Combine with ½ cup seedless raisins, ½ cup finely chopped nuts, ½ cup sugar and 1 teaspoon cinnamon.

Cherry: Spread 1½ cups finely ground nut meats over dough, cover with 4 cups canned sour red cherries, pitted and drained, and sprinkle with 1 cup sugar.

ETROG (CITRON) MARMALADE

Citron	Grapefruit
Orange	Sugar

Use 1 grapefruit and 1 orange to each citron available. Wash and dry the fruit. Peel the thin outside skin of the fruit and cut it into thin strips. Discard all the white pulp, the cores, and the seeds. Cut the fruit into coarse pieces, mix it with the strips of rind, and cover them in a kettle with three times as much water. Let the fruit stand overnight.

Boil the fruit and juice for 3 minutes, let it again stand overnight, then repeat the boiling process and again let it stand overnight. On the third day measure the fruit and juice, add an equal amount of sugar, and boil the mixture for 1 hour, or until it is thick. Pack and seal the marmalade in sterile jars.

PAREVE DESSERTS

NOTE: The availability on the market of vegetable gelatin (unflavored and flavored), of *pareve* vegetable margarine and of various soybean toppings which resemble whipped cream has made possible an almost unlimited variety of desserts suitable for meat as well as dairy meals. Here are a few:

ZABAGLIONE

4 eggs   2 tbsps. sugar
                    ½ cup sweet white wine

Beat the eggs in the top of a double boiler with a rotary beater until they are thoroughly blended. Add the sugar and wine; place the pan over hot but not boiling water, and continue to beat until the mixture is thick and fluffy. Serve warm in sherbet glasses. Serves 5.
VARIATION: Fruit juice may be substituted for the wine.

STRAWBERRY DELIGHT

Fresh whole strawberries   Orange juice
Sugar   Curaçao
                    Soybean topping

Wash and hull the berries, and sugar them lightly. Chill them in a mixture of equal amounts of orange juice and Curaçao; use just enough to moisten the berries well. Serve with soybean topping. (Quantities will depend on number to be served.)

CHOCOLATE MOUSSE

8-10 eggs (separated)   2 squares bitter chocolate
½ cup sugar   1 tsp. instant coffee
4 squares semi-sweet chocolate   1 tbsp. rum

Beat the egg yolks with the sugar. Combine and melt the semi-sweet and bitter chocolate. Add the melted chocolate, instant coffee and rum to the egg yolk and sugar mixture. Fold in the very stiffly beaten egg whites. Store in refrigerator for a couple of hours. Decorate with maraschino cherries. Serves 8 to 10.

MELON SURPRISE

1 large cantaloupe   1 package vegetable gelatin,
                                       strawberry or cherry
                    Water

Peel the melon and cut a thin slice off the bottom so that it stands firmly. Cut off approximately the top third of the melon and scoop out the seeds and pulp. Prepare fruit-flavored vegetable gelatin according to directions on package. When it is slightly thickened, pour the gelatin into the melon. Chill until the gelatin sets. If desired, garnish with grapes or cherries. Slice to serve. May be served with soybean topping.

HONEY APPLE BETTY

2 cups bread crumbs	¼ tsp. grated lemon rind
⅓ cup melted pareve margarine	1 tbsp. lemon juice
6 cups canned apple slices	2 tbsps. honey

Combine the bread crumbs and margarine, and arrange one-third of the mixture in the bottom of a greased casserole. Cover with half of the apples. Combine the cinnamon, lemon rind, lemon juice and honey. Spread half of this mixture over the apples. Cover with another third of the crumbs, the rest of the apples, and the remaining honey mixture. Sprinkle on the remaining crumbs. Bake in a 350° oven for about 1 hour, or until done. May be served with soybean topping. Serves 6.

BING CHERRY MOLD

1 can Bing cherries	½ cup granulated sugar
2 cups orange juice	2 packages lemon vegetable
1½ cups sherry	gelatin

Walnut or pecan halves

Mix the juice from the cherries with the orange juice, wine and sugar. Stir the mixture well, bring it to a boil, and dissolve the gelatin in it. When it begins to jell, pour half into a ring mold and arrange on it the cherries and nut meats. Pour in the remaining jelled mixture.

STRAWBERRY WHIP

1 unbeaten egg white	1 pint fresh strawberries

¾ cup powdered sugar *

Put aside several whole strawberries to top dessert. Wash, drain and crush the other berries. Put all ingredients in a bowl and beat until stiff. Serve on top of crumbled nutcake (or any leftover cake) which has been soaked for a half hour in wine. Or serve in sherbet dishes, topped with whole strawberries.

* This is a good Passover dessert if fine granulated sugar is used instead of powdered sugar, since powdered sugar contains cornstarch.

"It's a bad cook who doesn't lick her own fingers"
(English proverb)

RECIPE RAMBLINGS

Many traditional foods such as latkes, blintzes, or kreplach, prepared according to the dietary laws, are now commercially prepared and frozen.

Gefillte fish purchased in jars is quite satisfactory, when times does not allow making the homemade variety.

Bottled borscht and schav can be "improved" with the addition of eggs, sour cream or seasoning.

Excellent spongecake and nutcake mixes for Passover are now on the market.

Strudel leaves can be bought packaged, ready to be filled with your favorite filling and baked.

Cookie cutters in holiday symbol shapes can be found in Sisterhood gift shops and even some general toy stores. They make good gifts for the children.

Classes in Jewish cooking are given from time to time in large metropolitan cities.

Most of the manufacturers of Jewish foods have excellent menu and recipe pamphlets which they will send free on request.

Nationally known candy manufacturers now feature kosher and "pareve" cakes, candies, and confections in attractive packages, appropriate to the various holidays.

Attractive well-designed paper cloths, napkins, plates and cups, and table decorations with holiday symbols also are readily available.

TO HELP YOU COOK AND BAKE

THE JEWISH COOK BOOK by Mildred Grosberg Bellin (Bloch Publishing Company). International cooking according to the dietary laws. Thousands of traditional and many unusual recipes for Jewish dishes the world over.

THE ART OF JEWISH COOKING by Jennie Grossinger (Random House). Famous hotel owner gives her excellent recipes. Attractive format. Some menu suggestions.

JEWISH COOKERY by Leah Leonard (Crown). A good basic Jewish cookbook.

THE NEW JEWISH COOK BOOK by Betty Dean (Hebrew Publishing Company). Some Passover and other traditional dishes.

MOLLY GOLDBERG COOK BOOK by Molly Goldberg and Myra Waldo (Doubleday and Company). Molly's recipes with her own special "flavor." Comments on kashrut and Passover.

THE NEW SETTLEMENT COOK BOOK by Mrs. Simon Kander (Simon and Schuster). An excellent standard cookbook.

THE COMPLETE AMERICAN-JEWISH COOKBOOK, edited by Anne London and Bertha K. Bishov (World Publishing Company). Written "in accordance with Jewish dietary laws."

JEWISH HOME BEAUTIFUL by Betty Greenberg and Althea O. Silverman (Women's League). Holiday menus, recipes and table settings.

JEWISH HOLIDAY COOK BOOK by Leah Leonard (Crown). Menus and recipes for holidays and special occasions such as Bar Mitzvahs and weddings.

JEWISH FESTIVAL COOK BOOK by Fannie Engle and Gertrude Blair (David McKay Company). Sabbath and holiday menu suggestions and recipes, with interesting comments in a pleasant style.

JUNIOR JEWISH COOK BOOK by Aunt Fanny (Ktav Publishing Company). Cookbook for the youngster, with easy directions; attractively illustrated. Dietary laws, holiday recipes. Good gift book.

THE JEWISH HOLIDAYS AND THEIR FAVORITE FOODS by Fannie Engle (Behrman House). With charming illustrations by Dorothy M. Weiss. Easy recipes for mother and daughter.

THE ISRAELI COOK BOOK by Molly Bar David (Crown). 700 recipes of wide variety; oriental and Western Jewish cooking.

KOSHER COOKERY UNLIMITED by Ruth and Milton Perry (Women's League). With some dishes mother never knew.

KOSHER PARTIES UNLIMITED by Ruth and Milton Perry (Women's League). Glamour in the kosher kitchen.

Appendix

— 1 —

BOOKS FOR READING OR REFERENCE

"Books shall be thy companions; bookcases and shelves, thy pleasure nooks and gardens." (Judah Ibn Tibbon)

IN ADDITION TO the books on specific subjects listed in the text and at the end of each chapter, you might find the following listings helpful. They can be found in most libraries. Some you will want for your home library. This is by no means a complete or conclusive list. New books are being published all the time. Current newspaper and magazine reviews may suggest reading to you. The catalogs of the publishers listed on page 12 may also be helpful. The Jewish Book Council of America, New York, N. Y., publishes annotated lists of books in various categories. The Women's League and Hadassah have helpful book guides.

REFERENCE BOOKS

THE VOCABULARY OF JEWISH LIFE by Abraham Mayer Heller (Hebrew Publishing Company). Just what the title implies, an expanded glossary, with transliterated Hebrew words grouped in categories such as the home, synagogue, theology, learning. Good index.

THE STANDARD JEWISH ENCYCLOPEDIA, Cecil Roth, editor-in-chief (Doubleday). A popularly written, one volume modern encyclopedia of Jewish life.

JUNIOR JEWISH ENCYCLOPEDIA, edited by Naomi Ben-Asher and Hayim Leaf (Shengold Publishers). A reference guide for the family. Information on Jewish life and culture from ancient times to the present. Up to date and authoritative. Illustrated; easy to read. Attractive format.

BOOK OF JEWISH KNOWLEDGE by Nathan Ausubel (Crown). An encyclopedia of the Jewish people and Judaism, covering all elements of Jewish life from Biblical times to the present. 1000 illustrations.

SOME GENERAL BOOKS ON JEWISH BELIEFS AND PHILOSOPHY

GREAT AGES AND IDEAS OF THE JEWISH PEOPLE, edited by Leo Schwartz (Random House, for Hadassah). A series of essays by outstanding scholars.

THE GUIDE FOR THE PERPLEXED by Moses Maimonides (Dover). The unabridged text of the classic. An attempt to reconcile Judaism and Aristotelian philosophy.

THE KUZARI by Judah Halevi (Schocken Paperback). A basic book of Jewish literature. An argument for the faith of Israel by the foremost medieval Jewish poet and thinker.

JUDAISM: POST BIBLICAL AND TALMUDIC PERIOD edited by Salo W. Baron and Joseph L. Blau (Liberal Arts). A series of readings in basic Jewish writings, including the Apocrypha, Philo, Josephus, Talmudic writings, and prayers.

ASPECTS OF RABBINIC THEOLOGY by Solomon Schechter (Schocken Paperback). The main concepts of normative Judaism based on Talmudic thought.

MAJOR TRENDS IN JEWISH MYSTICISM by Gershom G. Scholem (Schocken, hardcover and paperback). Outline of the history of Jewish mysticism from its beginnings in antiquity to its latest phase in Hasidism.

BASIC JUDAISM by Milton Steinberg (Harcourt Brace). Clear, brief, well-organized statement of the beliefs, ideals and practices of the Jewish faith, in a compact, easy-to-read book.

WHAT THE JEWS BELIEVE by Philip S. Bernstein (Farrar,

Straus & Cudahy). A clear exposition of what the title suggests.

FAITH THROUGH REASON by Charles and Bertie G. Schwartz (Women's League). Ideals, principles and practices of Judaism as interpreted today, presented in clear and simple terms.

TRADITION AND CHANGE, edited by Rabbi Mordecai Waxman (Burning Bush Press). Essays on the development of Conservative Judaism.

THE STORY OF JUDAISM by Bernard J. Bamberger (Schocken Paperback). The author focuses on the inner content of Jewish life, the religious ideas, observances, and institutions.

THE WRITINGS OF MARTIN BUBER edited by Will Herberg (Meridian). A selection of essays interpreting the major doctrines of Buber's thought: human existence, social life, biblical faith, Jewish destiny, teaching and learning.

ISRAEL AND THE WORLD by Martin Buber (Schocken Paperback). Essays in a time of crisis.

FAITH AND REASON by Samuel Hugo Bergman (Schocken Paperback). An introduction to modern Jewish thought.

JUDAISM: A WAY OF LIFE by Samuel S. Cohon (Schocken Paperback). An introduction to the basic ideas of Judaism.

JUDAISM AS A CIVILIZATION by Mordecai Kaplan (Yoseloff). A presentation of the basic ideas of Reconstructionism.

WHAT IS THIS JEWISH HERITAGE? by Ludwig Lewisohn (Schocken Paperback). A selection of the writings of Lewisohn on the Jewish heritage.

ON HISTORY

A HISTORY OF THE JEWS by Solomon Grayzel (Jewish Publication Society). A popular one-column history of the Jews from the Babylonian exile to the present day.

A BIRD'S EYE VIEW OF JEWISH HISTORY by Cecil Roth (Union of American Hebrew Congregations. Also appeared under the title *History of the Jews* in a Schocken Paperback).

HISTORY OF THE JEWISH PEOPLE by Max Margolis and Alexander Marx (JPS-Meridian). A comprehensive history of the Jewish people from its beginnings to 1930.

THE GRAPHIC HISTORY OF THE JEWISH HERITAGE edited by P. Wolman-Tsamir (Shengold). Unusual encyclopedic presentation with maps, tables, and illustrations. Helpful to teenagers.

ANCIENT ISRAEL by Harry M. Orlinsky (Cornell). The story of the people and religion of Israel from their earliest beginnings to the Persian period.

THE DEAD SEA SCRIPTURES IN ENGLISH TRANSLATION translated and edited by Theodor H. Gaster (Doubleday-Anchor). A free translation of portions of the Dead Sea Scrolls.

JERUSALEM AND ROME: THE WRITINGS OF JOSEPHUS edited by Nahum N. Glatzer (Meridian). A selection of the writings of the First Century C. E. Jewish historian whose account of the struggle between Imperial Rome and the Jewish people is the chief contemporary source of information about Palestine in that period.

THE JEW IN THE MEDIEVAL WORLD by Jacob R. Marcus (JPS-Meridian). A presentation of documents that illuminate the world of the Jews in the Middle Ages.

MEMOIRS OF MY PEOPLE edited by Leo W. Schwarz (Schocken Paperback). Jewish self-portraits from the 11th to the 20th centuries.

JEWS IN AMERICA by Rufus Learsi (World Publishing Company). An authentic, readable one-volume history of the first 300 years of the Jews in America.

A HISTORY OF THE CONTEMPORARY JEWS FROM 1900 TO THE PRESENT by Solomon Grayzel (JPS-Meridian). A brief survey of the experiences and problems of the Jewish people during the past two centuries.

EUROPE AND THE JEWS by Malcolm Hay (Beacon). A history of anti-Semitism from the time of St. John Chrysostom to the founding of the State of Israel.

ON ISRAEL

THE DIARIES OF THEODOR HERZL edited by Marvin Lowenthal (Grosset and Dunlap). The diaries of the leading Zionist and founder of the State of Israel.

THE ZIONIST IDEA edited by Arthur Hertzberg (JPS-Meridian). An anthology of important writings on Zionism with an essay on the subject by the author.

FULFILLMENT: THE EPIC STORY OF ZIONISM by Rufus Learsi (World Publishing Company). The history of the Zionist movement and Israel up to 1951.

ISRAEL: ITS ROLE IN CIVILIZATION, edited by Moshe Davis (Jewish Theological Seminary). Essays on Israel's position in the modern world; the political, religious, cultural life of the new state.

KIBBUTZ: VENTURE IN UTOPIA by Melford E. Spiro (Schocken, hardcover and paperback). The daily life, attitudes, and problems of the collective settlement in Israel.

ISRAEL by Joan Comay and Moshe Pearlman, with an introduction by Golda Meir (Macmillan). A profile of Israel from
Biblical to modern times.

JEWISH LIFE AND LITERATURE

A JEWISH READER edited by Nahum N. Glatzer (Schocken, hardcover and paperback). Sourcebook of post-biblical Jewish literature, theology, faith, philosophy, folklore, practical law.

LIFE IS WITH PEOPLE by Mark Zborowski and Elizabeth Herzog.
Introduction by Margaret Mead (Schocken Paperback). The culture of the *Shtetl.*

THE HASIDIC ANTHOLOGY edited by Louis I. Newman (Schocken
Paperback). A lexicon of Hasidic teachings.

TALES OF THE HASIDIM by Martin Buber (Schocken, hardcover
and paperback). Stories of the masters of the impassioned movement which swept Eastern European Jewry in the 18th century. In
two volumes.

TEN RUNGS: HASIDIC SAYINGS by Martin Buber (Schocken, hardcover and paperback).

A TREASURY OF YIDDISH STORIES edited by Irving Howe and
Eliezer Greenberg (Meridian). An anthology of Yiddish short
stories translated into English.

YIDDISH PROVERBS edited by Hanan J. Ayalti, illustrations by
Bernard Reder (Schocken, hardcover and paperback).

ISRAELI STORIES edited by Joel Blocker (Schocken). Selection of
the best writing in Israel today.

BURNING LIGHTS by Bella and Marc Chagall (Schocken, hardcover and paperback). A double portrait of a childhood in Vitebsk.
Text by Bella Chagall with thirty-six of Marc Chagall's drawings.

THE GREAT FAIR: SCENES FROM MY CHILDHOOD by Sholom
Aleichem (Noonday). An autobiographical novel of the author's
experiences as a growing boy in a small town in Russia.

SATAN IN GORAY by Isaac Bashevis Singer (Noonday). The effect
of Sabbatai Zevi on the Jewish population of Goray, a Polish
hamlet.

RÖYTE POMERANTSEN by Immanuel Olsvanger (Schocken). Classic selection of Jewish humor told in Yiddish and printed in the Roman alphabet.

IN THE HEART OF THE SEAS by S. Y. Agnon (Schocken). A short novel describing a pilgrimage of early 19th century Polish Hasidim to Palestine.

TO HELP YOU HELP YOUR CHILDREN

WHEN YOUR CHILD ASKS—A Handbook for Parents, by Simon Glustrom (Bloch Publishing Company). Questions children frequently ask. Simple and helpful answers suggested, on God, holidays, practices, death.

YOUR CHILD AND YOU, a series of pamphlets for Jewish parents (United Synagogue Commission on Jewish Education). Subjects covered include bringing up the Jewish child, Jewish education at home, Bar Mitzvah, Bat Mitzvah, etc.

LET'S TALK ABOUT GOD

LET'S TALK ABOUT JUDAISM

LET'S TALK ABOUT RIGHT AND WRONG

by Dorothy Kripke (Behrman House). These three very attractive books will be helpful in answering children's questions. Intelligent and imaginative simple conversational stories. Delightful illustrations.

ONE GOD—THE WAYS WE WORSHIP HIM by Florence Mary Fitch (Lothrop, Lee and Shepard). The story of Judaism, Protestantism and Catholicism simply presented, to help children (from 10 to 14) understand religions other than their own. Good photographs.

NOTE: There are many excellent books for children to read and enjoy. These can be checked through your Sisterhood gift and book shops as well as through Jewish and general bookstores.

BLESSINGS

"It is a good thing to give thanks unto the Lord" (Psalms 92.2)

Blessings for various ceremonies and occasions will be found in your siddur and in Count Your Blessings (Women's League). The following are most frequently used in the home. Although transliterations are included, they are not recommended for regular use; they should lead to a resolve to study the original Hebrew.

FOR FOOD AND WINE

❧ **ON BREAKING BREAD**

בָּרוּךְ אַתָּה יְיָ אֱלֹהֵינוּ מֶלֶךְ הָעוֹלָם הַמּוֹצִיא לֶחֶם מִן הָאָרֶץ:

baruḥ atah adonai elohenu meleḥ ha'olam, hamotzi leḥem min ha'retz

Blessed art Thou, O Lord our God, King of the universe, Who brings forth bread from the earth.

❧ **ON DRINKING WINE**

בָּרוּךְ אַתָּה יְיָ אֱלֹהֵינוּ מֶלֶךְ הָעוֹלָם בּוֹרֵא פְּרִי הַגָּפֶן:

baruḥ atah adonai elohenu meleḥ ha'olam, bore peri hagafen.

Blessed art Thou, O Lord our God, King of the universe, Who creates the fruit of the vine.

Note—the full kiddush for Sabbath and Festivals will be found in your prayer book.

CANDLE LIGHTING

❧ ON THE SABBATH EVE

בָּרוּךְ אַתָּה יְיָ אֱלֹהֵינוּ מֶלֶךְ הָעוֹלָם אֲשֶׁר קִדְּשָׁנוּ בְּמִצְוֹתָיו וְצִוָּנוּ
לְהַדְלִיק נֵר שֶׁל שַׁבָּת:

baruḥ atah adonai elohenu meleḥ ha'olam, asher kideshanu
bemitzvotav vetzivanu l'hadlik ner shel shabbat.

Blessed art Thou, O Lord our God, King of the universe, Who has
sanctified us by Thy commandments, and instructed us to kindle
the Sabbath lights.

❧ ON ROSH HASHANAH AND THE THREE FESTIVALS

בָּרוּךְ אַתָּה יְיָ אֱלֹהֵינוּ מֶלֶךְ הָעוֹלָם אֲשֶׁר קִדְּשָׁנוּ בְּמִצְוֹתָיו וְצִוָּנוּ
לְהַדְלִיק נֵר שֶׁל [שַׁבָּת וְשֶׁל] יוֹם טוֹב:

baruḥ atah adonai elohenu meleḥ ha'olam asher kideshanu
bemitzvotav, vetzivanu lehadlik ner shel [shabbat ve] yom tov.

Blessed art Thou, O Lord our God, King of the universe, Who has
sanctified us by Thy commandments and instructed us to kindle
the [Sabbath and] Festival lights.

❧ ON YOM KIPPUR

בָּרוּךְ אַתָּה יְיָ אֱלֹהֵינוּ מֶלֶךְ הָעוֹלָם אֲשֶׁר קִדְּשָׁנוּ בְּמִצְוֹתָיו וְצִוָּנוּ
לְהַדְלִיק נֵר שֶׁל [שַׁבָּת וְשֶׁל] יוֹם הַכִּפּוּרִים:

baruḥ atah adonai elohenu meleḥ ha'olam asher kideshanu
bemitzvotav vetzivanu lehadlik ner shel [Shabbat ve] yom hakip-
purim.

Blessed art Thou, O Lord our God, King of the universe, Who has
sanctified us by Thy commandments and instructed us to kindle
the [Sabbath and] Yom Kippur lights.

Note—If the Festival or Holy Day coincides with a Friday evening,

add the words in brackets. On the first night of a Festival, add
sheheheyanu (below).

❧ ON KINDLING THE HANUKKAH LIGHTS

בָּרוּךְ אַתָּה יְיָ אֱלֹהֵינוּ מֶלֶךְ הָעוֹלָם אֲשֶׁר קִדְּשָׁנוּ בְּמִצְוֹתָיו וְצִוָּנוּ
לְהַדְלִיק נֵר שֶׁל חֲנֻכָּה:

baruḥ atah adonai elohenu meleḥ ha'olam asher kideshanu
bemitzvotav vetzivanu lehadlik ner shel Hanukkah.

Blessed art Thou, O Lord our God, King of the universe, Who has
sanctified us by Thy commandments and instructed us to kindle
the lights of Hanukkah.

בָּרוּךְ אַתָּה יְיָ אֱלֹהֵינוּ מֶלֶךְ הָעוֹלָם שֶׁעָשָׂה נִסִּים לַאֲבוֹתֵינוּ בַּיָּמִים
הָהֵם בַּזְּמַן הַזֶּה:

baruḥ atah adonai elohenu meleḥ ha'olam she'asah nissim la'-
avotenu bayamim hahem bazeman hazeh.

Blessed art Thou, O Lord our God, King of the universe, who has
performed miracles for our fathers in days of old, at this season.

NOTE: On the first evening, add *sheheheyanu* (below)

SHEHEHEYANU

בָּרוּךְ אַתָּה יְיָ אֱלֹהֵינוּ מֶלֶךְ הָעוֹלָם שֶׁהֶחֱיָנוּ וְקִיְּמָנוּ וְהִגִּיעָנוּ לַזְּמַן
הַזֶּה:

baruḥ atah adonai elohenu meleḥ ha'olam, sheheheyanu vekiye-
manu vehigiyanu lazeman hazeh.

Blessed art Thou, O Lord our God, King of the universe, Who has
kept us in life, preserved us and enabled us to reach this season.

ON WASHING HANDS BEFORE MEALS

בָּרוּךְ אַתָּה יְיָ אֱלֹהֵינוּ מֶלֶךְ הָעוֹלָם אֲשֶׁר קִדְּשָׁנוּ בְּמִצְוֹתָיו וְצִוָּנוּ
עַל נְטִילַת יָדַיִם:

Blessed art Thou, O Lord our God, King of the universe, Who has sanctified us by Thy commandments and instructed us concerning the washing of hands.

ERUV TAVSHILLIN

בָּרוּךְ אַתָּה יְיָ אֱלֹהֵינוּ מֶלֶךְ הָעוֹלָם אֲשֶׁר קִדְּשָׁנוּ בְּמִצְוֹתָיו וְצִוָּנוּ
עַל מִצְוַת עֵרוּב:

Blessed art Thou, O Lord our God, King of the universe, who has sanctified us by Thy commandments, and instructed us concerning the *eruv*.

בְּהֲדֵין עֵרוּבָא יְהֵא שָׁרֵא לָנָא לְמֵיפָא וּלְבַשָּׁלָא וּלְאַטְמָנָא
וּלְאַדְלָקָא שְׁרָגָא וּלְמֶעְבַּד כָּל־צָרְכָּנָא מִיּוֹמָא טָבָא לְשַׁבְּתָא
לָנוּ וּלְכָל־הַדָּרִים בָּעִיר הַזֹּאת:

By virtue of this *eruv*, be it permitted us to bake, cook, keep food warm, kindle lights and do all the work that is necessary on the Festival for the Sabbath, to us and to all the House of Israel that dwell in this city.

ON SEPARATION OF THE DOUGH OR TAKING OF HALLAH

בָּרוּךְ אַתָּה יְיָ אֱלֹהֵינוּ מֶלֶךְ הָעוֹלָם אֲשֶׁר קִדְּשָׁנוּ בְּמִצְוֹתָיו וְצִוָּנוּ
לְהַפְרִישׁ חַלָּה:

Blessed art Thou, O Lord our God, King of the universe, Who has sanctified us by Thy commandments, and commanded us concerning the separation of the dough.

GLOSSARY

THIS MODEST but adequate glossary represents an attempt to aid the reader in a practical, down to earth way; without the distractions of "etymology," encyclopedic paragraphs, or a rehash of the entire contents of the book. Here, as in the text, Hebrew transliterations are italicized, Yiddish is quoted, and words that have gained general usage in English are set conventionally.

alav hashalom—Phrase used after the name of a deceased person. Means "Peace upon him." Feminine form: *aleha hashalom*.

aliyah—Literally, ascent; the honor of being called to the Torah-reading in the synagogue. Also used in other contexts, for example, settling in the land of Israel.

amidah—A central portion of each daily service. Literally: standing; it is recited standing and in silence.

amud—Lectern in the synagogue.

arba kanfot—The small fringed prayer-garment worn beneath the outer garments. Also called *tallit katan*.

aron hakodesh—The holy ark containing the scrolls of the Torah in the synagogue.

Asarah Betevet—The tenth day of Tevet—minor fast.

"aufruf"—The custom of calling a prospective bridegroom to the Torah.

avodah—A section of the Yom Kippur service.

ba'al tefillah—Lay reader at public worship.

ba'al tekiah—One skilled in sounding the shofar.

"balabosteh"—A Jewish housewife; the word carries complimentary overtones.

Bar Mitzvah—The status of religious responsibility reached by a Jewish boy when he becomes thirteen years old. Current usage applies the term to the celebration of this new status.

Bat Mitzvah—The status of religious responsibility reached by a girl at the age of twelve; see Bar Mitzvah.

bedikat ḥametz—The search for leaven; a home ritual for the night before Passover eve.

ben—son.

beraḥah—A blessing; plural, *beraḥot.*

bet hakenesset—The synagogue.

bet hamidrash—The house of study; applied to the synagogue, as well as to an academy.

bet hatefillah—The house of prayer.

besamim—The spices used at the *havdallah* ceremony.

bimah—The raised dais in the synagogue from which the Torah is read.

birkat hamazon—The grace after meals.

brit milah—The circumcision ceremony. Literally: the covenant of circumcision.

"dreidel"—A Ḥanukkah spinning top for children to play with.

erev—Literally: evening. Applied to the day before a holy day, as when Friday is called "erev Shabbat."

Eretz Israel—The land of Israel. (Hebrew: *eretz yisrael.*)

eshet ḥayyil—A woman of valor; first words of the poem at the end of the Book of Proverbs.

etrog—A citron, used ceremonially on Sukkot; plural, *etrogim.*

etz ḥayyim—Tree of life; term used for the wooden handles attached to the Torah scroll.

"fleishig"—Describes food which contains meat or meat derivatives.

gemar ḥatimah tovah—New Year greeting for use after Rosh Hashanah.

Gemarah—A voluminous work based on the Mishnah; the two together make up the Talmud.

geshem—The prayer for rain recited on Shemini Atzeret.

get—The religious document of divorce.

"gut voch"—Greeting after *havdallah:* Happy Week.

Haftarah—The passage from the Prophets read in the synagogue after the reading of the Torah.

Haggadah—The book containing the Seder service for Passover eve.

hag same'ah—Happy holiday; a form of greeting.

hakafot—Processions in the synagogue on Sukkot, but especially on Simhat Torah.

hallah—White loaf used on Sabbath and festivals. Plural *hallot*.

Hallel—Psalms of praise (Psalms 113-118) recited on festive days.

halutzim—Pioneers in the land of Israel.

hametz—Leaven; food prohibited on Passover.

Hamishah Asar Bishevat—The fifteenth day of the month of Shevat, celebrating the first signs of spring in the land of Israel; also called the New Year of the Trees.

hamotzi—The blessing for bread; hence, grace before meals.

hanerot halalu—The opening words of a meditation recited after lighting the Hanukkah candles.

Hanukkah—The Feast of Dedication, also called the Feast of Lights and the Feast of the Maccabees.

haroset—A condiment used at Seder to symbolize the mortar used by the slave in Egypt.

Hassidim—Followers of Hassidism, a movement in Judaism originating in the eighteenth century. Emphasizes the emotional aspect of religion. The adjective is: Hassidic.

hatan bereshit—The person who is called to the reading of the first chapter of Genesis on Simhat Torah.

hatan torah—The person called to the reading of the last sentences of the Torah on Simhat Torah.

havdallah—The ceremony for the departure of the Sabbath.

hazzan—Cantor.

hillul hashem—The desecration of God's name; a term applied to disgraceful behavior.

hol hamo'ed—The intermediate days of Passover and of Sukkot.

hora—A folk dance of East European origin associated with modern Israel.

hoshana—Rubric of prayers recited on Sukkot. Also applied to the willow twigs attached to the *lulav* which are used separately on the seventh day of Sukkot.

Hoshana Rabbah—The seventh day of Sukkot.

ḥumash—The first five books of the Bible; i.e., the Five Books of the Torah, often called the Pentateuch.

ḥuppah—Marriage canopy.

kabbalat shabbat—Welcoming the Sabbath; the service that precedes the regular evening service on Friday night.

Kaddish—A doxology recited at public worship. In the form called Mourners' Kaddish it is said by the bereaved.

karpas—The herb, usually parsley, dipped in salt water at the Seder.

"kasher"—To make kosher; Yiddish verb derived from Hebrew.

kashrut—The Jewish dietary laws.

kedushah—A responsive profession of faith chanted at public worship.

Keren Hayesod—Israel Foundation Fund, now incorporated into UJA.

kriah —Ceremonial rending of a garment by mourners.

ketubah—The Jewish marriage contract.

ketuvim—The Hagiographa; name given to the third division of the Hebrew Bible, from Psalms to Chronicles.

kiddush—Invocation of the sanctity of a holy day, recited primarily in the home before meals, and preferably with wine.

kiddushin—One name for the marriage ceremony.

kinot—Liturgy for Tishah B'Av.

kohelet—The Book of Ecclesiastes in the Bible.

kohen—A descendent of the priestly family of Aaron; plural *kohanim*.

Kol Nidre—Chanted at the beginning of the service on Yom Kippur eve.

kosher—According to the Jewish dietary laws.

"kvatter"—Godfather at circumcision.

"kvatterin"—Godmother at circumcision.

Lag Ba'omer—Thirty-third day (of the counting) of the Omer; Scholar's Festival.

leḥah dodi—A sixteenth century Sabbath eve hymn.

leshanah haba'ah biyerushalayim—Next year in Jerusalem.

leshanah tovah tikatevu—"May you be inscribed for a good year"; greeting on Rosh Hashanah.

lu'aḥ—A Jewish calendar.

lulav—Palm branch bound with the myrtle and the willow; used on Sukkot.

ma'ariv—The evening service.
ma'asim tovim—Good deeds.
Maftir—The person called to read the concluding passage of the Torah portion; also the passage itself.
Magen David—The six-pointed star which, in recent centuries, has gained acceptance as a Jewish symbol.
mah nishtanah—The opening words of the four questions asked by a young child at the Passover Seder.
Mahzor—Holy day prayer book.
ma'ot hittim—Traditional Passover fund for the needy.
Ma'oz Tzur—A Hanukkah hymn.
matzah—Unleavened bread; plural, *matzot*.
mazal tov—Congratulations!
megillah—Scroll; plural, *megillot;* megillat Esther—book of Esther.
melaveh malkah—A feast of farewell to the Sabbath.
Menorah—Candelabrum.
mezuzah—Small parchment with Biblical passages attached to the door-post. Plural, *mezuzot*.
"milchig"—Dairy; foods containing milk products.
minyan—The quorum of ten males over the age of thirteen, required for public worship.
minhah—The afternoon service.
mi sheberah—A short prayer offered on behalf of one who has been called to the Torah.
Mishnah—A work, completed about 200 C.E. which codifies Jewish oral tradition since the Torah. It is the basic part of the Talmud.
mitzvah—Commandment. Plural, *mitzvot*. In popular speech, it has come to mean a good deed.
mo'adim lesimhah—Greeting on the Three Festivals.
mohel—One qualified to perform ritual circumcision.
musaf—An additional element in the morning service on Sabbaths, Festivals, and the New Moon.

ne'ilah—The concluding service on Yom Kippur.
ner tamid—The Eternal Light over the Torah ark.
nevi'im—Prophets.

omer—Originally a measure of grain; applied to the counting of 49 days between Passover and Shavuot.

Oneg Shabbat—The peaceful joy which the Sabbath should bring. Applied in modern times to informal social gatherings on the Sabbath, usually of a cultural nature.

parashah—One of the 54 portions into which the Torah is divided for the annual cycle of scripture readings. Plural, *parashot*. Also called *sidrah*, plural: *sidrot*.

"pareve"—Neutral; foods containing neither milk nor meat products. For example, vegetables.

Pesach—The Festival of Passover.

pidyon haben—Redemption of the first born. (A ceremony held on the 31st day after the birth of certain baby boys when the conditions described on page 34 obtain.)

Pirke Avot—A tractate of the Mishnah, often called "Ethics of the Fathers."

pittum—The nodule at the tip of an *etrog*.

parohet—The curtain of the ark in which the Torah scrolls are kept in the synagogue.

Purim—The Feast of Esther.

refu'ah shelemah—A get-well wish; literally, "a complete recovery."

Rosh Hashanah—The New Year in the Jewish religious calendar.

Rosh Hodesh—New Moon; the beginning of each month in the Hebrew calendar.

sandek—The man who holds the baby during the circumcision.

Sanhedrin—The High Court in ancient Israel.

Seder—The service conducted at the meal on Passover eve.

Sefer Torah—A scroll of the Torah.

sefirah—Counting the days from Passover to Shavuot; hence the period itself. Full name, *sefirat ha'omer*.

sehah—The herbage used as a roof for the Sukkah.

selihot—Prayers of penitence; particularly those recited at midnight in anticipation of Rosh Hashanah.

se'udah—A festive meal.

shaddai—Almighty; word inscribed on the mezuzah.

shaharit—The morning service.

"Shalach Monos"—Gifts exchanged on Purim; from the Hebrew *mishlo'ah manot.*

"Shalosh Se'udos"—The snack, usually accompanied by group singing, taken just before the end of the Sabbath. The Yiddish derives from the Hebrew *shalosh se'udot*—"three meals"; more properly *se'udah shelishit*—"the third meal."

shamash—Attendant. The term is applied to the sexton of the synagogue; and also to the extra candle on Hanukkah, the "servant of the light."

Shavuot—One of the Three Festivals; known as Pentecost and as The Feast of Weeks.

shavu'a tov—Good week; greeting at the termination of the Sabbath. Yiddish equivalent: "gut voch."

sheheheyanu—The benediction reserved for special occasions; named for its key word.

shehitah—Ritual slaughter of animals for food.

sheloshim—The 30 days of mourning following bereavement.

shema—The paragraph in the Bible that starts with "Hear O Israel." (Deuteronomy 6:4-9)

Shemini Atzeret—The eighth day of Sukkot.

sheva berahot—A portion of the marriage service also included in grace after the wedding feast.

shir hashirim—The Biblical Song of Songs.

shivah—The seven days of full mourning immediately following bereavement.

Shivah Asar Betammuz—Fast of the 17th of Tammuz.

shofar—The ram's horn sounded on the High Holy Days. The plural, *shofarot*, is also applied to a portion of the Rosh Hashanah service.

shohet—One qualified to slaughter animals and fowl for kosher food.

Shulchan Aruch—Comprehensive code of Jewish law, compiled by Joseph Caro of Safed in the sixteenth century.

Shushan Purim—The day after Purim.

Siddur—A prayer book.

sidrah—See *parashah.*

simhah—Any joyful occasion, like a wedding. Plural, *simhot.*

Simhat Torah—The festive day, at the end of Sukkot, when the annual cycle of Torah readings is completed and begun over again.

sukkah—A temporary hut or booth used during the Festival of Sukkot.

Sukkot—The Feast of Tabernacles.

taharah—The word means purification; may be applied to the rules governing marital relations, as well as to other contexts.

taḥriḥim—Shrouds.

tal—Prayer for dew recited on the second day of Passover.

tallit—A prayer shawl.

Talmud—The major repository of post-Biblical Jewish law and tradition. Consists of the Mishnah and the Gemara.

tanaḥ—The Bible; the Holy Scriptures.

tashliḥ—A ceremony conducted on the afternoon of Rosh Hashanah at the shore of a body of water.

tefillin—Phylacteries.

Tishah B'Av—The fast on the ninth day of the month of Av.

Torah—The Pentateuch, more broadly, all Jewish learning and tradition.

trefah—Non-kosher; forbidden food.

Tu Bishevat—A modern Israeli name for Hamishah Asar Bishevat, which see.

tzedakah—The current word for charity; but its root meaning is "righteousness."

tzitzit—Fringes on the corners of the tallit (Numbers 15.38).

Tzom Gedaliah—The Fast of Gedaliah, Tishri 3rd.

yad—The pointer used by the reader of the Torah.

"yahrzeit"—The anniversary of death.

yizkor—Prayers of memorial recited on the last day of each of the Three Festivals, as well as on Yom Kippur.

yom tov—Any Jewish festival day.

"yomtovdik"—Festive.

zemirot—Songs; particularly the hymns sung at the Sabbath table.

Zohar—The most widely known book of Jewish mysticism.

INDEX